P9-CRE-506

8 Fl Gr

Young People's Science Encyclopedia

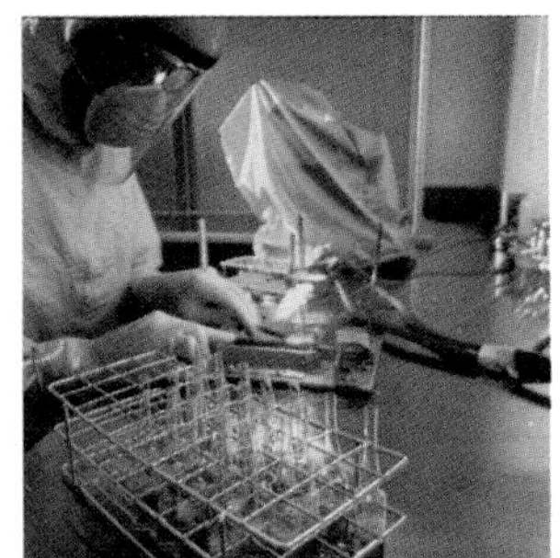

YOUNG PEOPLE'S SCIENCE ENCYCLOPEDIA

Young People's SCIENCE Encyclopedia

Edited by the Staff of

NATIONAL COLLEGE OF EDUCATION

Evanston, Illinois

Volume 8/Fl-Gr

CHICAGO

Photographs

Page 2: Skylab space station (NASA)

Page 3: *Top to Bottom:*
Wheatfield (U.S.D.A. Photo)
Technician capping Abbokinase (Abbott Laboratories)
Spider (Macmillan Science Company)
View of Earth (NASA)
Space Shuttle (NASA)
Bahama coral reef (Macmillan Science Company)

Cover: Design by Sandra Gelak
Lake Clark (National Park Service)
Giraffe (Milwaukee County Zoo)
Green Frog (James P. Rowan)

Library of Congress Catalog Card Number: 67-17925

California flying fish sometimes come in near shore

Flying fish These fish are gliders rather than fliers. They do not move their wings when in the air. Their wings are large fins near the head. Usually these fish fly close to the surface of the sea and may average 35 miles (56.33 kilometers) an hour. Often they fly to avoid being eaten by larger fish like tuna or mackerel.

Tails are adapted for flight. They are two lobed with the lower lobe longer. To become airborne, the fish swims upward rapidly. As it leaves the water surface, the long lower tail lobe beats back and forth (about 50 beats per second) in the surface water. The beating gives the fish more lift. As momentum is lost, the fish drops back to the water surface.

Some flying fish have four wings. The posterior and anterior are both enlarged. These fish also glide. The freshwater South American hatchet fish do have true flight, but they are not in the same order as the marine flying fish. These belong to the order Synentognathi and the family Exocoetidae.

Eggs have long threads to hold them to floating objects. Young fish have long feelers beside the mouth. They may be longer than the fish and are lost at maturity. J. C. K.

SEE ALSO: PISCES

Flying saucer see Unidentified flying objects

FM (Frequency Modulation) see Radio

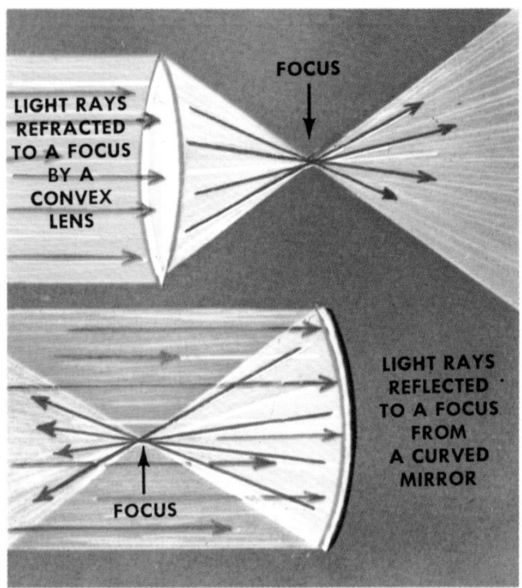

Light rays reflect or refract to a focus

Focus The focus is the point at which waves of sound, rays of LIGHT, or rays of heat meet, or would meet if there were no interference. In particular, it is the point where the rays meet after they have been reflected or refracted. It is also the point from which such waves start and spread out. In GEOLOGY, the focus is the place where an EARTHQUAKE starts. In medicine, focus is the place where a disease starts or where it is concentrated.

SEE: LENS, MAN-MADE; OPTOMETRY

Foetus see Fetus

Fog Fog is a cloud that is near or touching the surface of the Earth. Like many clouds, fog is made of tiny droplets of liquid water that has condensed from water vapor.

Fog is formed as the air close to the surface of the Earth is cooled in some manner. The way in which the air is cooled will cause the formation of one of two types of fog—*radiation* or *advection* fog. Radiation fogs are caused by the rapid loss of heat of the Earth and cooling of the air above it. Advection fogs are the result of warm, moist air moving into areas of colder air. H. S. G.

SEE ALSO: WEATHER

✳ THINGS TO DO

WHAT CAUSES FOG?

1. **Fill a bottle one-third full of hot water. Place a piece of ice over the mouth of the bottle.**
2. **After several minutes observe what happens above the surface of the water.**
3. **As the warm moist air rises it hits the cool air under the ice. The molecules of water come together to form minute drops. This is fog. Eventually these small droplets would form larger ones and fall as rain.**

Folding Folding is the process by which portions of the earth's crust are bent so that each side extends down from, or up from, the fold point. Some MOUNTAINS and valleys are created by folding.

SEE: GEOLOGY

Foliage see Leaves

Courtesy Society For Visual Education, Inc.

Folding of the earth's crust

Ripe milkweed follicles split open to allow the wind to disperse the silky-haired seeds

Courtesy Society For Visual Education, Inc.

Follicle (botanical) (FAL-uh-kuhl) A follicle is a dry fruit that holds seeds. It has one compartment, and a seam, or suture, along one side that splits when the SEEDS are ripe.

A milkweed pod is a good example of a follicle. It opens the way a book opens. Legume or pea pods differ from follicle pods by the way they open. Legumes open along seams on both sides of the pod.

The fruit of peonies, monkshood, and larkspur are classified as follicles. M. R. L.

SEE ALSO: PEONY, LEGUME, SEED DISPERSAL

Follicle (reproductive) A follicle is a tiny secretory sac of gland cells. The *Graafian* follicle, for example, is the small spherical sac which contains the EGG cell and secretes a hormone.

SEE: MENSTRUATION, REPRODUCTIVE SYSTEMS

Food see Malnutrition, Nutrition

Food chain This is the passing of food energy from plants to animals. The first link is the producer or green plant such as algae. The first-level consumer could be a daphnia that eats the algae which is in turn eaten by a hydra. Food chains are short, usually only three or four links. Only about 20% of the energy is passed on to the next level.

A *food web* is a series of interconnected food chains. For example, clover may be eaten by a field mouse which in turn may be eaten by an owl, weasel, or hawk; in turn, a hawk may eat a weasel. Or, clover may be eaten by a cow which in turn may be eaten by humans.

A *food pyramid* displays the energy levels and the number of organisms that occupy each level. It takes a tremendous amount of BIOMASS at the bottom to support a few at the top. It could take 30,000 pounds (13,607.76 kilograms) to produce 3,000 pounds (1360.78 kilograms) of beef to feed a 130-pound (58.97-kilogram) person. An aquatic food pyramid shows that it takes 600 pounds (272.16 kilograms) of plankton to produce a few pounds (kilograms) of herring to produce an ounce (a few grams) of tuna.

Humans may be forced to eat more plants instead of meat. This is due to the fact that it takes 10 acres (4 hectares) to raise a beef cow for market. In contrast, with a crop of soybeans 500 pounds (227 kilograms) of protein can be produced on 1 acre (.4 hectare). H.J.C.

Food preservation If it were not for food preservation, there would not be strawberries in January or fresh peas in December. One would have to journey to Hawaii if one wanted pineapple or to Maine for lobster. Food preservation enables man to set aside part of the foods he raises and therefore to have a safe, year-round diet of many kinds of fruits, vegetables, and meats. Food preservation helps to prevent food from spoiling.

Food spoils for two reasons: (1) presence of microorganisms, and (2) chemical changes. Some microorganisms help plants and animals to live, but when the plant or animal dies, other tiny, living things speed up the process of rotting. Chemical substances called ENZYMES cause chemical changes in raw foods. In ripened fruit, the enzymes continue to work after the fruit is picked and will cause decay unless the fruit is preserved. Blanching, PASTEURIZATION, STERILIZATION, freezing, dehydrating or using harmless chemical preservatives will destroy or slow down the microorganisms and enzymes.

From the earliest times, mankind has known of ways to preserve food. Some historians say that cave man smoked meat in order to keep it for the lean months of hunting. The ancient Egyptians knew that grain keeps for a long time in dry, cool storehouses; that adding salt to fish or meat keeps it from rotting; that drying in the sun also keeps meat or fish edible for long periods. For centuries food has been preserved by using sugar, spices, vinegar, and brine.

Many of these methods of preserving are used today for some foods, but there are also modern, scientific processes of canning, freezing, and dehydration. Food processing has become an enormous business, the largest manufacturing industry in the United States. Properly preserved food may be sent safely to people all over the world, or it may go from the backyard garden to the freezer and eventually to the family dinner table. J.K.K.

SEE ALSO: DEHYDRATION, REFRIGERATION

Food pyramid see Food chain

Food vacuole see Protozoa

Foot see Measurement, Skeleton

Foot and mouth disease see Animal diseases

Foot-candle see Candela

Foot-pound The foot-pound is the most frequently used unit for measuring WORK OR ENERGY when the *pound* is the unit of force. Work is done to move an object from one place to another or to stop or speed up a moving object. Force is what is required to start the object moving or to stop it. The work done depends upon the amount of force, the distance through which the force is applied, and the direction of the force with respect to the displacement.

One may write

$$W = F \times d$$

where F is the force in pounds and d is the distance in feet through which the force acts. Thus if an object weighing one pound were lifted through a distance of one foot, one foot-pound of work would be done.

When very large forces are present, the *foot-ton* is sometimes used. Any combination of force and distance units may be used in describing work and energy. H. W. M.

SEE ALSO: FORCES, MEASUREMENT

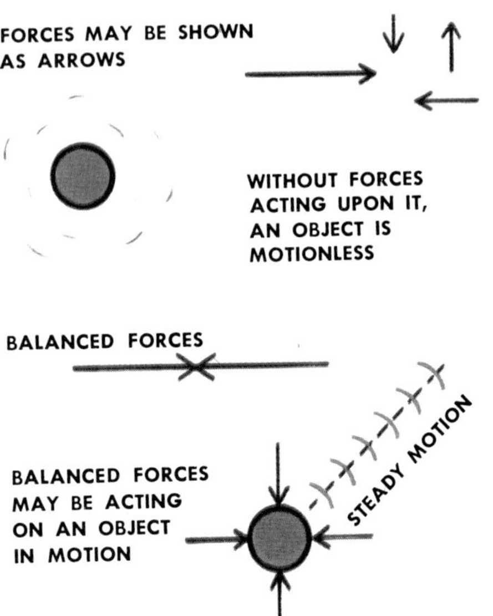

Force arm see Machines, simple

Forces A force is a push or pull in any direction exerted on some object. The force may or may not move the object. The laws controlling force are part of the laws of motion developed by Sir Isaac Newton.

Newton's Laws of Motion state that:

1. A body at rest stays at rest unless acted upon by an external force, and a body remains in motion with uniform velocity and in a straight line unless acted on by an external force.
2. The acceleration of a body is proportional to the force that caused the body to move and is in the same direction as the force. The acceleration is inversely proportional to the mass of the body.
3. For every action there is an equal and opposite reaction.

In Newton's Second Law of Motion an absolute standard is used to measure the force, as in the formula:

$$F = ma \text{ or } a = \frac{F}{m}$$

which means that the resulting acceleration is directly proportional to the force and inversely proportional to the mass. This can be illustrated using a spring balance hooked to a small car. If the force is doubled, the acceleration is doubled, and if the mass is doubled, the acceleration is cut in half. FRICTION is not taken into account.

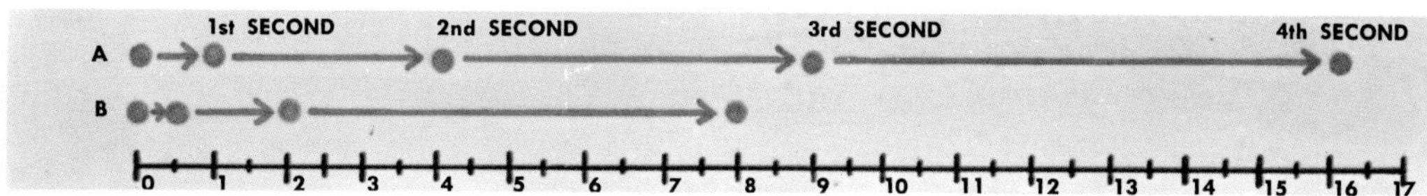

Acceleration means speeding up. The same force keeps acting on an object. As seen above, A has two times as much force acting on it as B has. If B had twice as much mass as A, twice as much force would be needed in order for it to accelerate at the same rate as A

Newton's Third Law of Motion may be well expressed as the interaction of forces that are equal but opposite in direction. This is illustrated in the following:

If a boy in a boat pushed a floating log toward the shore with a certain force, the boat will be pushed away from the shore with exactly the same force.

The composition of two or more forces acting on a point gives a single *resultant force* which has the same total effect as the combination of the other forces. This is shown in the following diagram:

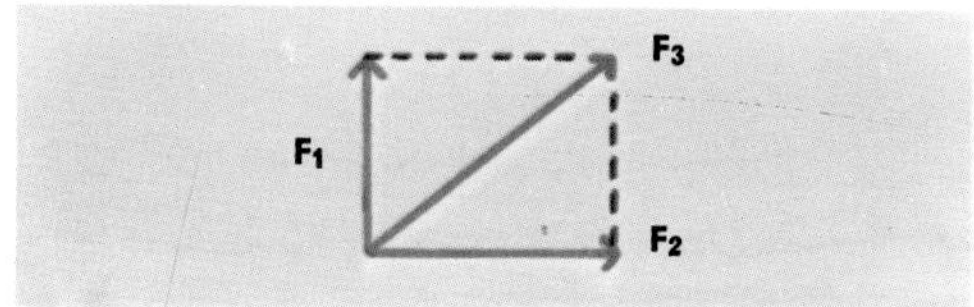

where F_1 and F_2 are the individual forces with a resultant force, F_3. Another illustration is given in the following:

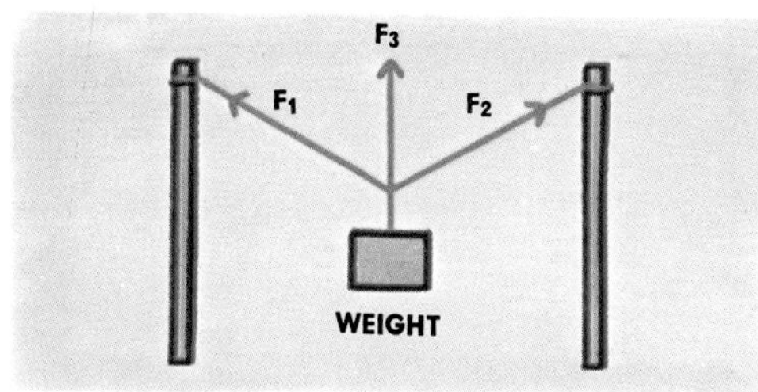

The composition of forces F_1 and F_2 produces a third force, F_3, equal and opposite to the weight of the object.

Most of the methods of measuring forces involve choosing units for length, mass and time. By definition a unit of force called the *dyne* measures force in the *cgs* system (centimeter-gram-second). According to the *mks* system (meter-kilogram-second), the unit of force is measured in *newtons,* in honor of Sir Isaac Newton. The newton is defined as that force applied to one kilogram which will give it an acceleration of one meter per second squared. One newton is equal to 100,000 dynes.

The Boeing Company

A jet-propelled aircraft functions according to Newton's Third Law of Motion. The thrust of gas out the back pushes the craft forward

In the *fps* (*foot-pound-second*) system, instead of defining force in terms of mass, the reverse is done. An object that has a weight *W* pounds due to the gravitational acceleration *g* feet per second per second is defined as having a mass of W/g *slugs.* This changes the relationship of

$$F = ma \qquad \text{to} \qquad F = \frac{W}{g}\,a$$

Other than forces produced by man and his environment, there are four major known forces existing in Nature. These are: (1) force caused as the result of the attraction of two or more masses; (2) force caused by the mutual attraction or repulsion of two or more electrical charges; (3) force caused by the attraction or repulsion of two or more magnetic fields; (4) nuclear forces, present at or near the surface of the nucleus of all atoms. This nuclear force only operates over very short distances, but it is much greater than any one of the other three major forces.

E. Y. K.

SEE ALSO: ACCELERATION, DYNAMICS, GRAVITY, MASS, MECHANICS, MOMENTUM

Forecast see Weather forecasting

Forest, Lee de see DeForest, Lee

Forest preserve see Preserves

✳ **THINGS TO DO**

STARTING FOREST TREES IN THE HOME OR CLASSROOM

1. **Collect seeds from a variety of trees—ash, maple, pine, oak, elm and others.**
2. **Soak the seeds for a day to help loosen the seed coats.**
3. **Plant the seeds several inches apart in a woodland terrarium or pots of rich garden soil. (See Terrarium to make a woodland one.) Keep them well watered.**
4. **The seeds with a thinner coat will germinate and grow faster. It takes time for the seed in an acorn to break through the thick coat and appear.**
5. **As soon as the young saplings are several inches tall they may be planted outside.**
6. **Put a wire cylinder around them the first year or two to prevent animals from stepping on them. Water and fertilize when needed.**

Forest products Since the earliest times, the forest has been man's great friend. It gave him food, shelter and clothing. Wood was man's first fuel. Leaves were perhaps his first dishes and also made a roof over his head. Early man used the floating log for transportation, but wherever he traveled he still needed the forest and its products.

For thousands of years, the gums of certain small trees and shrubs have been used to produce frankincense and myrrh. These are valuable RESINS which are still in demand for incense, PERFUME, ANTISEPTICS, and embalming. Medicines and DYES were distilled from bark, roots and stems of other woody plants. Early trade and exploration was dependent upon ships of wood. Aside from the need of wood for practical purposes, lumber of sandalwood, EBONY and TEAK were used to beautify the environment. Found among the jewels of primitive man was AMBER, the petrified or fossil resin of a certain pine.

In the Middle Ages, metal workers and glassmakers lived in or near the forest to be close to the source of supply for FUEL. By this time, charcoal furnaces had long been in use. Man was able to convert HARDWOODS into charcoal to produce greater heat. The making of CHARCOAL was perhaps man's first chemical process.

In the present time, the use of the forest is virtually unlimited. The most obvious use is wood for all kinds of building purposes from boxes to bridges. The manufacture of VENEER, PLYWOOD, roofing and railroad ties constitute a vast industry. Demand for lumber still makes the biggest inroads in the forest, but science has discovered many uses for former waste products. No part of the tree is unused. Sawdust is converted into fuel briquettes, soil conditioners, artificial woods, composition floors and insulation. Countless PAPER products are made almost entirely from pulpwood.

CELLULOSE, a carbohydrate present in the cell walls of plants, is another valuable by-product of the sawmill. From cellulose was obtained *celluloid,* the first PLASTIC. Other cellulose derivatives are rayons, plastics, artificial leathers, varnishes, FILM, cellophane and EXPLOSIVES. Cellulose or wood HYDROLYSIS produces a range of materials from acetic acid, alcohol, glycerine, medicines, bleaches, wood sugars to cattle food.

Latex, gums and resins are various wood secretions. The demand for RUBBER made from latex cannot be over-estimated. Resin products include rosin, waterproofing, soaps and linoleum. Pioneer children chewed the gummy sap of spruce and pine, but today, chewing gum manufacturing rests upon the use of CHICLE, obtained from the gum of the sapodilla tree.

Tannin, found chiefly in bark, is the ingredient that turns stiff animal hides into strong flexible leather. Tannin is also employed in the making of medicines and inks. QUININE, chalmoogra oil and dyes are bark and root products of trees. The bark of still another tree is CORK.

Less obvious, but definitely on the list of valuable forest products, are COAL and PETROLEUM, both having organic origins in prehistoric times. These are sources for materials such as NYLON, COKE, AMMONIA, gasoline, PARAFFIN, petroleum jelly and kerosene. PEAT is a semi-carbonized fiber that is used for fuel and soil-conditioning.

The number of uses that man finds for wood is constantly increasing, as is seen in the chart on the following page. The scientific renewal and harvesting of the forest go on continuously. In addition to the products of the forest, man gains the important side benefits of soil-erosion prevention, control of water supply and creation of animal refuge and recreation areas. J. A. D.

SEE ALSO: ECONOMIC BOTANY, FORESTRY

Woods commonly used in furniture and other household items are important forest products

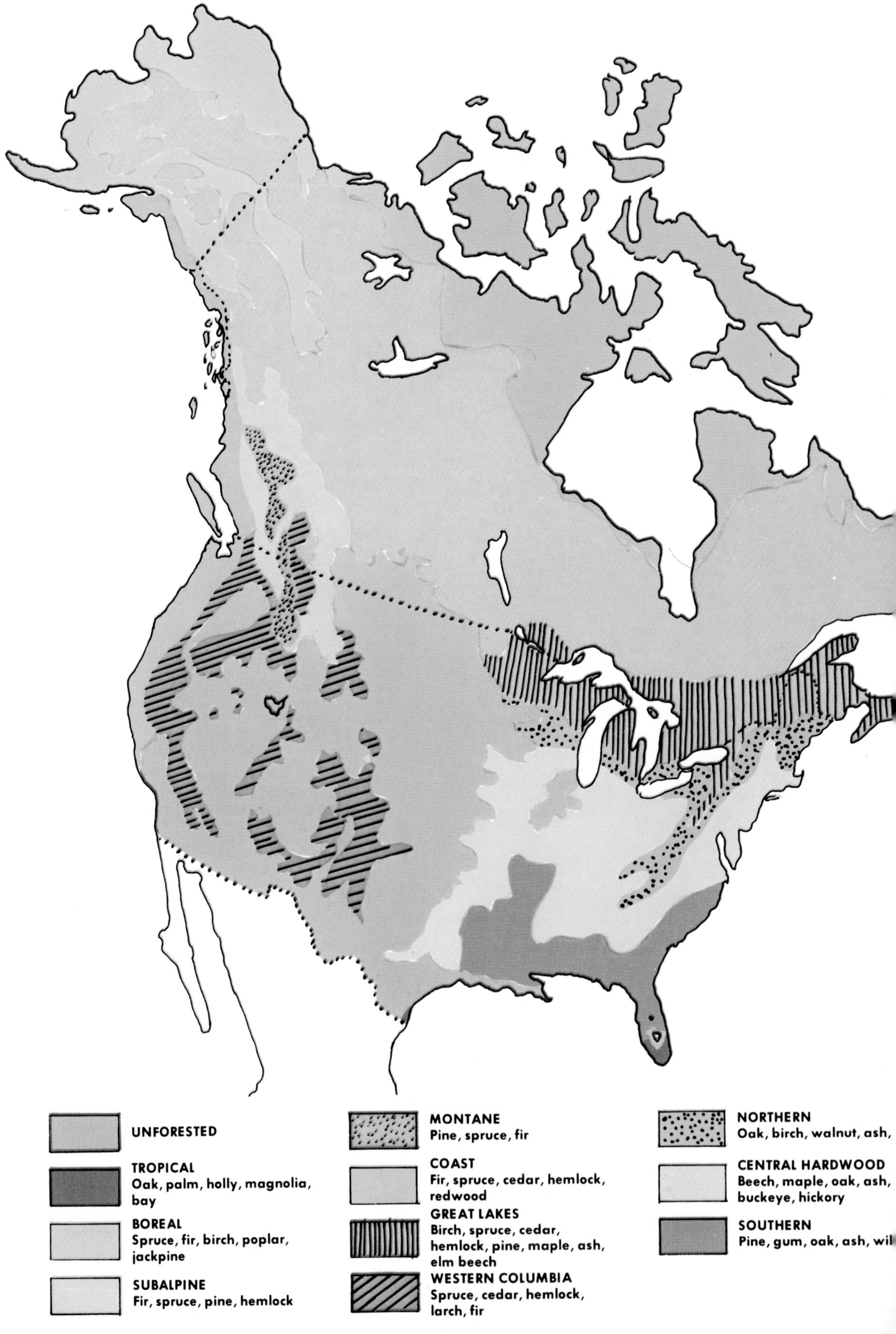

UNFORESTED

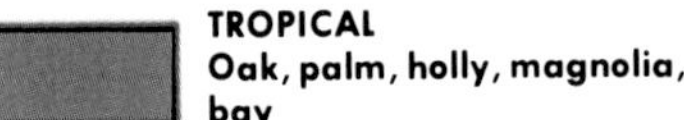
TROPICAL
Oak, palm, holly, magnolia, bay

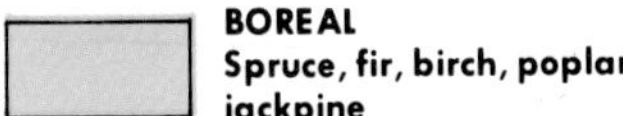
BOREAL
Spruce, fir, birch, poplar, jackpine

SUBALPINE
Fir, spruce, pine, hemlock

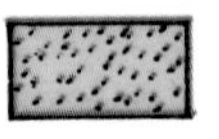
MONTANE
Pine, spruce, fir

COAST
Fir, spruce, cedar, hemlock, redwood

GREAT LAKES
Birch, spruce, cedar, hemlock, pine, maple, ash, elm beech

WESTERN COLUMBIA
Spruce, cedar, hemlock, larch, fir

NORTHERN
Oak, birch, walnut, ash,

CENTRAL HARDWOOD
Beech, maple, oak, ash, buckeye, hickory

SOUTHERN
Pine, gum, oak, ash, wil

FOREST PRODUCTS AND THEIR USES

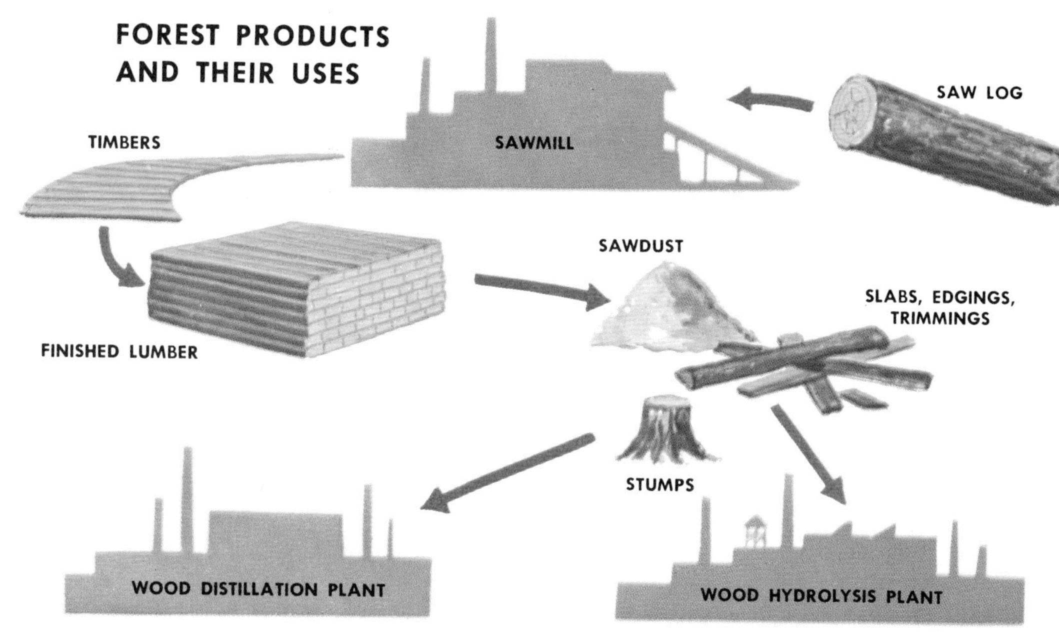

PRODUCTS	USES
ACETIC ACID	Solvent, acetate for rayon, photographic film, perfumes, dyes, paints
CHARCOAL	Fuel, explosives, chemicals, drugs, water purification
SOLVENTS, OILS AND TARS 	Solvents—lacquers and paints Oils and tars—disinfectants, dyes, medicines, rope, paints
TURPENTINE 	Paint and varnish, synthetic camphor for celluloid
ROSIN 	Varnish, soap, waterproofing, linoleum, greases

PRODUCTS	USES
CARBONIC ACID	Industrial chemicals
ANIMAL FOOD	For cattle and poultry
GLYCERINE	Medicines, industrial chemicals
BUTADIENE	Synthetic rubber
METHYL ALCOHOL	Solvents
SUGARS	Animal feed, alcohol

Practically no part of a cut tree is wasted. Among other types of wood-processing plants are plywood and veneer mills. These produce thin sheets of wood, often highly polished, used in furniture and boats. Even an ice-cream stick is a type of veneer! Another kind of factory is the hardboard plant, which uses chips, flakes, and limbs. These are made into hardboard and particle board, which are used for soundproofing and in building construction

OTHER PRODUCTS

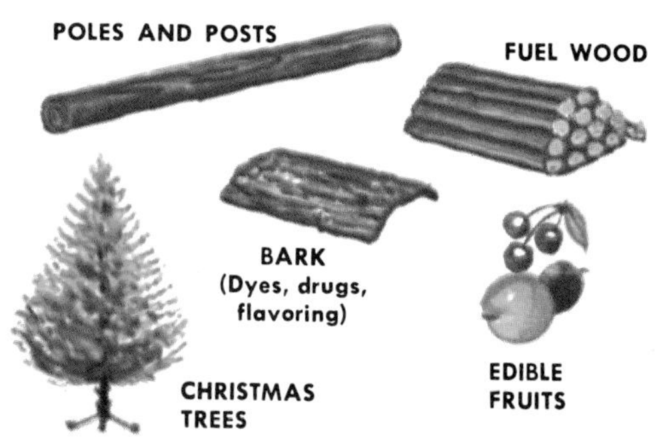

Forestry A forest is more than a group of trees. It is a whole community of living things. Growing under trees are shrubs, herbs, lower plants, and tiny life in the soil. A forest is the home for many kinds of animals. Forestry is the study and care of all the living organisms in this particular environment.

There were over 950 million acres (384,451,700 hectares) of forests in America in the 1600s. Currently that number has dropped to around 600 million acres (242,811,600 hectares) in the United States. However, Canadian forest reserves are tremendous. It has over a billion acres (404,686,000 million hectares). Canada is the largest exporter of timber in the world. The United States imports almost half of what is cut, averaging around 4 billion cubic feet (113 million cubic meters) annually.

In 1876 Congress appointed the first special forestry agent. In 1891 the first national forest was created. There are over 150 of them in the United States today. Thousands of local, state, and federal people are employed in the science of forestry.

KINDS OF FORESTS

The boreal or *coniferous* forests grow in a wide band all along the northern part of the United States and up to the arctic tundra. Since the climate is cold, the growing season is rather short. The trees in this type of forest include redwood, pine, fir, cedar, spruce, larch, tamarack, and live oak.

The temperate or hardwood forests extend across the center of the country. The climate is neither extremely cold nor hot. The *deciduous* and conifer trees are exposed to seasonal changes. These stands of trees are among the oldest on the continent. The forests are often a combination of two kinds of trees, such as maple and beech or hickory and oak. Other trees include ash, gum, and locust.

The southern evergreen forests extend from Virginia to Florida and across to Texas. The climate is wet and warm. The trees native to this area are magnolia, bald cypress, water oak, pitch pine, and gum.

The southern tip of Florida and parts of Mexico are not true rain forests but are closely related in the types of vegetation that thrive there. The rainfall is heavy and the temperature high. The broadleaf trees are evergreen and grow so tall and thick that little sunlight filters through. The undergrowth is limited. Air plants flourish.

CARE AND MANAGEMENT OF TIMBER

How fast does a tree grow? It is estimated that an acre (hectare) of trees will produce 55 cubic feet (1.56 cubic meters) of timber annually. It is projected that by 2000 America will consume almost 100 billion board feet (240 million cubic meters). Conservation of this natural resource can be accomplished by following certain guidelines. Only the most mature trees should be selected and cut down. Inventories made from aerial photographs aid in this selection. Block or strip harvesting is the removing of small sections at a time.

As trees are cut and removed, new ones must be planted. Over rough terrain airplanes are used to sow tree seeds. On level ground a seeding machine can plant 10 acres (4.05 hectares) daily. Fertilizer and

Planned forests are protected from destruction by misuse, fire, and natural enemies. On the left are tree stumps from misused timberland and an area reforested with young firs and pines. From the nearby fire control tower, forest rangers keep constant watch. When a fire is located, help is sent. On the right, two men dig a firebreak to prevent a fire from spreading.

weed killer can be applied at the same time. Young, year-old seedlings are subject to adverse weather conditions and pests. Planting young trees takes longer, but the survival rate is higher. There are now over 35,000 private tree farmers, and demand for lumber continues to grow.

A division of the Forest Service is responsible for fire protection plans. This involves studying fire history, surveying cover types, organizing good maps, setting up watersheds, and laying out communication lines. Towers and stations in strategic spots make daily observations of the dryness of vegetation, the relative humidity, and the wind direction and velocity. This is recorded on a fire-danger meter as a burning index.

Plant disease is the number one killer, taking a toll of 20 billion board feet (48 million cubic meters) per year. The most serious diseases are oak wilt, Dutch elm disease, white pine rust, chestnut blight, and various mildews and mold rots. Insects are the number two killers, destroying over 8 million board feet (19.2 million cubic meters) annually. They may attack any part of the tree. If they do not kill the tree, they slow growth and weaken the wood. White grubs damage roots. Pine weevils, aphids, and sawflies eat buds and twigs. Japanese beetles, cankerworms, various webworms, caterpillars, and leaf miners feast upon the leaves. Many species of borers and beetles live beneath the bark. The need for better insecticides and methods of application is great.

CURRENT RESEARCH IN FORESTRY

Scientists experiment on such problems as wood preservation, timber physics and mechanics, wood chemistry, pulp and paper manufacture, milling methods, and disease control. The study of thermodynamics has led to better fire-fighting techniques. The effect of wind speed, humidity, and amount of heat given off from certain woods are researched by conducting miniature forest fires in a laboratory. Experimentation on pollution has disclosed that hardwoods withstand polluted air far better than do softwoods. This information leads to wiser restoration of wooded land near industrial areas. Balloons and helicopters are being used to airlift logs and whole trees. This eliminates the massive machinery which does damage to the entire environment of a forest area.

The science of reforestation is an important aspect in basic forestry. The concept of tolerance revolves around particular characteristics a tree inherits. How much shade or sun can it tolerate? What temperature is necessary for maximum growth? Can the soil be acid or alkaline, compacted or porous, deep or shallow, wet or dry? All these conditions must be examined before new forests can be started or burned-out areas can be replanted.

Continual vigilance, money, and effort are required to maintain and replenish this valuable natural resource. The demands on our forest lands will be tremendous. H.J.C.

SEE ALSO: CONSERVATION OF NATURE, FOREST PRODUCTS, PRESERVES, RIVER

Forget-me-nots

Forget-me-not The color of the FLOWERS on this herb is most often blue. Some kinds may be pink or white. The long slender stem is quite hairy. The LEAVES are long and simple.

The inflorescence on the flower stalk forms a one-sided cluster. Each flower has five petals, sepals, and stamens. The pistil is composed of two united carpels. It develops into a fruit of four one-seeded nutlets.

The PERENNIAL forget-me-not has flowers in May and June. The ANNUAL variety, about 9 inches (22.86 centimeters) high, flowers from June to August. The Chinese variety is a BIENNIAL about 2 feet (.61 meters) tall.

This herb is sometimes called mouse-ear because of its tiny leaves. Forget-me-nots are members of the family Boraginaceae. H. J. C.

Forging (FORE-jing) Forging is the shaping of metals by hammering. A piece of METAL is heated to a certain temperature and then either hand hammered or power hammered depending on its size.

Formaldehyde (for-MAL-duh-hide) Formaldehyde is a chemical COMPOUND. It is a gas and it has a strong, stinging odor. In water solution, it is used as a DISINFECTANT, an INSECTICIDE, and a PRESERVATIVE.

When the gas is dissolved in water to 40 percent strength, it is called *formalin.* Formalin is commonly diluted to 10 percent with water or alcohol, and it is used as a preservative of biological specimens. Continued exposure to formaldehyde can cause serious irritation to human skin, nose, and eye tissues.

Industrially, formaldehyde is valuable in making certain PLASTICS and ADHESIVES. It also helps produce wrinkle-proof cloth and wet-strength paper. It is an organic compound with the formula HCHO. D.A.B.

Formula A formula is the name of a pure material in standard chemical signs. Each element has a symbol, which is an abbreviation of its name. It is a type of "shorthand."

A formula includes the symbol of each element which the material contains. It also includes numbers written below the line following the symbol of the element to which they refer. The number indicates how many parts of that element are present in the material, or how many atoms of the element are present in the molecule. Sulfuric acid is made up of two parts of hydrogen (symbol H), one part sulfur (S), and four parts oxygen (O). The formula of sulfuric acid is H_2SO_4.

Structural formulas and models help to explain differences in chemical properties between substances of the same composition

```
   H  H  H  H
   |  |  |  |
H—C—C—C—C—H is butane,
   |  |  |  |
   H  H  H  H
```

```
   H  H  H
   |  |  |
H—C—C—C—H, isobutane.
   |  |  |
   H  |  H
      |
   H—C—H
      |
      H
```

In organic CHEMISTRY a *structural formula* is often used. The way in which the atoms are joined is shown by lines connecting their symbols. This is necessary to indicate exactly what material is being discussed. For example, the formula C_4H_{10} might be butane or isobutane, depending upon the arrangement of atoms. If two carbon atoms hold three hydrogen atoms apiece, and two hold two hydrogen atoms, the material is butane. However, if three carbon atoms held three hydrogen atoms apiece and the fourth held only one, it would be isobutane. The difference is shown in a structural formula.

J. K. L.

SEE ALSO: ORGANIC COMPOUNDS

Forsythia (for-SITH-ee-uh) This is a flowering shrub which blooms in early spring. The yellow FLOWERS are in the shape of a bell at their base. The four petals are not united, however, at the other end. The flower buds open up several weeks before the leaf buds. The flowers may be single or in clusters of two to four.

The LEAVES of forsythia are simple and arranged opposite from each other on the slender stems. Their margins are saw-toothed (serrated) and the venation is pinnate. The branches of this bush have a tendency to droop. If permitted to grow without pruning, branches will extend over 9 feet (2.74 meters). Forsythia is easily propagated from stem cuttings. Natural PROPAGATION may occur by fragmentation. If the branches come in contact with the soil, roots may form at a node. After sufficient growth this new plant can be severed from the "mother" shrub. It is a member of the Oleaceae family.

H.J.C.

Forsythia Courtesy Society For Visual Education, Inc.

Fossil fuels PETROLEUM, COAL, and NATURAL GAS are the most important fossil fuels in use in the world today. As a group, fossil fuels currently produce more of the world's energy than all other sources combined. Fossil fuels are the remains of organisms that lived up to hundreds of millions of years ago. After the organisms died, they were eventually covered by layers of sedimentary ROCKS.

Much of the world's petroleum is found trapped between layers of rock formed during the CENOZOIC ERA, which began about 65 million years ago. Petroleum is made up of long chains of HYDROCARBONS which were formed as organic matter decomposed in the absence of oxygen. Natural gas is closely related to petroleum and is usually found near petroleum deposits. Natural gas is composed of short chains of hydrocarbons, mostly METHANE. Coal is the oldest of the fossil fuels. Many coal deposits are found in rocks dating back to the Carboniferous Age (roughly 350 million to 280 million years ago).

Fossil fuels release heat energy when they are burned. During OXIDATION, carbon atoms from the fuel join oxygen atoms from the air to form CARBON DIOXIDE gas. Depending on the type and purity of the fuel, small or large amounts of other pollutants are also produced. The burning of fossil fuels is a major cause of increasing levels of carbon dioxide gas in earth's atmosphere, a condition that many scientists believe may lead to global warming.

J.H.

SEE ALSO: ENERGY CRISIS, GREENHOUSE EFFECT

Fossils Scientists who study the rocks, minerals, landforms, and the history of the earth can tell what kind of plants and animals lived on the earth a long time ago. These scientists are called *geologists.* One way that they are able to do this is by the study of fossils. Fossils may be the actual remains of plants or animals, impressions of them in rock, or the tracks of animals as they walked or crawled.

Most fossils are formed in the waters covering the continental shelves, in warm, shallow, inland seas, and in large swamps that covered large parts of the land in past geologic time. When the animals of these waters die, their remains are deposited on the floor of the water body where the fleshy part of the animal decays. The skeletal portion of the body is partially replaced by minerals and other sediments. If this takes place in just the right manner, a fossil is formed. Since rock sediments are involved in the formation of fossils, it is not surprising that one finds many fossils in sedimentary rock layers. Plant fossils are found in the areas that were once swamps.

There are four principal kinds of fossils: original remains, replaced remains, molds and casts, and impressions.

ORIGINAL REMAINS

In some instances, fossils represent the actual remains of plants and animals. Entire bodies of the woolly MAMMOTH, the elephant-like creature of an early era called the Pleistocene Age, have been found almost perfectly preserved in the perpetually frozen earth of Siberia. Why they died and were instantly frozen is still a mystery.

On the shores of the Baltic Sea in Europe, insects of millions of years ago have been found perfectly preserved in the hardened resin of pine trees upon which they crawled. This hardened resin is called AMBER. Other examples of original remains are the shells of shellfish which become consolidated or pressed together to form fossil varieties of limestone, and the bones and teeth of DINOSAURS and other ancient animals.

Another type of original remains may be found at Rancho La Brea, near Los Angeles, California, where there are ASPHALT pits containing the bones of thousands of animals. They were caught while looking for water or trying to cross the oil-covered lakes of asphalt. As they cried out in their death struggle, their enemies were attracted to the sticky mass and also trapped. Then the bodies sank down into the asphalt. Animals were also trapped in peat bogs like the ones at Big Bone Lick, Kentucky. Some were caught in quicksand. Both plants and animals have been buried by volcanic ash and lava, as well as by wind-blown dust and sand.

Minerals replaced the wood in petrified trees

REPLACED REMAINS

Many fossils no longer contain the original materials of which they were made, although they may look unchanged. Ground water may replace the lime shells and bones with such hard minerals as silica and iron pyrite. The petrified trees of Arizona are an example of this formation. They were formed when ground water slowly replaced the decaying wood of these buried trees with silica.

Sometimes all of an animal or plant has disappeared except for the CARBON in its body. In this way, carbon films of leaves, jellyfish, worms, and a few reptiles have been preserved.

Fossil molds are all that remains of animals and fish that have become extinct.

MOLDS AND CASTS

Sometimes a fossil shell or bone is completely dissolved out of the rock in which it was preserved. This leaves a hollow mold which shows only what the shape of the fossil had been. The filling of such a mold with new mineral material may produce a cast of the original fossil plant or animal. Molds and casts of shellfish are common fossils. The molds of ferns, leaves, and fish are also found in many rocks.

IMPRESSIONS

Impressions found in the muds and sands of flood plains and deltas by moving animals may be preserved when the sediments become rock. In shales and sandstones, geologists have found the footprints of dinosaurs, the trails of ancient worms, and the many other impressions of things living in the past.

All pictures Chicago Natural History Museum

The history of this fossil began as a skeleton 30 million years ago (1). A nearby river flooded (2), then receded, leaving a layer of sediment (3). For thousands of years more sediment built up and hardened over the fossilizing skeleton (4). The land dried and erosion began 30 thousand years ago (5). The index fossil is finally discovered in modern times (6)

INDEX FOSSILS

The large majority of fossils are found in deposits of sediment carried by water. After a long time this sediment changes to rock.

Sedimentary ROCKS are found in layers. These layers of rock and the fossils in them can be used to trace the history of the earth and its living things. Geologists know that different layers of rock were formed at different times. Of course, the oldest layers were formed first, the newest ones last, and the others in the ages between.

By studying the fossils in the different layers of rock, from the oldest to the newest, one can see along with the geologist many changes that have occurred in living plants and animals. Some kinds of fossils appear in several different layers, while other kinds are found only in layers formed during a certain time in the earth's history. When geologists find a layer of rock with these fossils in it, they can tell not only which layer it is but also about when it was formed. Fossils help geologists separate the history of the earth into various divisions of time. These fossils are called *index fossils* because they help correlate the geological histories of the different continents.

Index fossils are a great aid to the oil geologist. He knows that many oil deposits have been found in the rocks of a particular geologic period. In seeking new oil deposits

✳ THINGS TO DO

HOW WERE FOSSIL IMPRINTS FORMED?

1 Prepare a mixture of cement, sand, water, and lime. This is similar to sandstone—a sedimentary rock which contains many fossils. Pour this into a shallow box cover.

2 Just before it sets press a shell, a leaf, or an animal's foot (dog's paw) into the surface of the mixture. Permit the mixture to harden.

3 Another way of making fossils is done with clay and plaster of Paris. Push modeling clay into a shallow cardboard box. Smooth the surface.

4 Push different parts of organic objects into the clay and remove them.

5 Make a mixture of plaster of paris and water to the consistency of thick soup. Pour this over the clay and let it set.

6 Remove the cardboard box and clay from the plaster mold. A fossil is imprinted on the plaster.

he uses his knowledge of the index fossils of this period in helping him identify other formations of the same geologic period.

Not only do fossil remains show what kinds of plants and animals lived in the past, they also indicate what the climate and other conditions were like when these animals and plants were alive. Woolly mammoths and woolly rhinoceroses lived during a time of ice and extreme cold. Today, ferns grow mostly in warm, moist places. Fossil ferns probably had a warm climate and grew near wet marshy places. Corals are now found only in warm, shallow, salt water. It is likely that fossil corals lived in oceans of this kind. Sedimentary rocks often contain fossil imprints of raindrops, ripples of water, and mud cracks. These show what conditions on the earth were probably like during the time of formation of these fossils.

FOSSIL PLANTS

According to the fossil record, the first known plants were mostly green, blue-green, red, and brown ALGAE. It is possible that BACTERIA and DIATOMS also existed. The first land plants began to grow about 350,000,000 years ago according to the estimate of geologists. About 250,000,000 years ago, the FERNS that attained great height came. The remains of these ferns are in coal deposits. Finally, during the Devonian period, the seedbearing plants appeared and eventually became the main form of plant life on earth.

Fossil molds of leaf fronds found in shale.

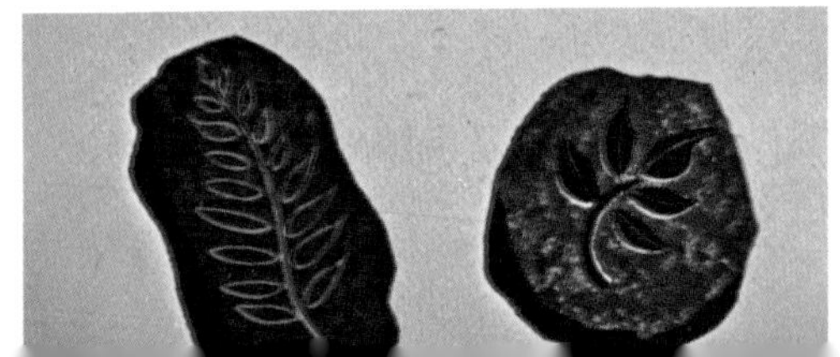

Chicago Natural History Museum

Three-toed horses about 30,000,000 B.C., known from fossil skeletons

FOSSIL ANIMALS

Fossils have been found of INVERTEBRATE animals that appear to be approximately 600,000,000 years old. MOLLUSCA and TRILOBITES have been discovered in sediment up to 570,000,000 years old. Land animals appear to have developed approximately 500,000,000 years ago. Fossilized evidence of primitive insects and fish is up to 400,000,000 years old.

In 1991, 200,000,000-year-old DINOSAUR fossils were found in Antarctica. The discovery proved that the giant reptiles once lived on every continent of the world. Flying reptiles, birds, and the first mammals appeared from 190,000,000 to 150,000,000 years ago. PRIMATES began to appear about 65,000,000 million years ago. The oldest primate fossils resembling human beings are just a few million years old.

Fossils are found throughout the world. One of the most famous and productive sites is the La Brea tar pits in Los Angeles. There, prehistoric animals, including saber-toothed tigers and huge bears, were trapped and fossilized by asphalt sludge lurking beneath their drinking water. The La Brea tar pits is the only active urban fossil dig currently open to the public in the U.S. During the summer of 1992, a total of 1,117 fossil specimens were pulled out of La Brea's Pit 91 by volunteer excavators.

Collecting fossils, especially those of large animals, has become big business. In 1990, a team of excavators from Montana State's Museum of the Rockies dug up the fossilized skeleton of a Tyrannosaurus Rex. A Japanese firm later offered to buy it for four million U.S. dollars. In late 1992, some companies were selling fossilized skeletons of common dinosaurs for hundreds of thousands of dollars. A single dinosaur tooth, depending on its quality, could be purchased for about twenty dollars. J.H./V.V.N.

SEE ALSO: ANTHROPOLOGY, EVOLUTION, EVOLUTION OF MAN, PALEONTOLOGY

Chicago Natural History Museum

A zebra of the American plains that lived one million years ago

Founding Founding is the process of melting METAL and pouring it into a mold to shape it. The mold is usually made of sand and the metals shaped in this way include iron, STEEL, brass, bronze and aluminum.

Four-o'clock The FLOWERS on this bushy herb open up late in the afternoon. The bloom may be yellow, white, or shades of red. The LEAVES are simple and part of the flower turns into a dry FRUIT.

Each flower is perfect, having both male and female structures. It is incomplete because there are no petals. The colored tube or calyx is composed of five fused sepals. Green bracts surround the base of the calyx. Each flower has five stamens and one pistil with a single carpel. The indehiscent fruit is an anthocarp. The plant grows 3-5 feet (.91-1.52 meters) high and is thus suitable for hedges or borders of gardens and yards. H.J.C.

Four o'clocks have many clusters of trumpet-like flowers

Fowl Fowl is a name for any bird. It is commonly used to describe any bird —wild or domesticated—eaten by man. Fowl produce meat, eggs, and sometimes feathers for man's use. Some fowl, such as the wild duck, goose, and turkey, are hunted for these products, but a large majority of these birds are domesticated, or raised in captivity. Their characteristics can be changed by cross-breeding so that some lay superior eggs, others produce quality meat, and others grow soft or decorative feathers.

Cochin hen (left) and the little bantam

The CHICKEN is a domesticated fowl that is very useful to man. There are many breeds of chickens being raised throughout the world. They differ in size, color, markings, shape of comb, ability to lay eggs, quality and quantity of flesh, and resistance to disease. Some breeds have been developed especially for their egg-laying ability, while others have been developed for their meat. The breeds called the *Minorca* (more common in Europe than in the United States) and the *leghorn* are especially good egg layers. The *Plymouth Rock* is a heavy chicken and furnishes much meat. Still others have been developed for their ability to fight. Cock fighting is an ancient sport that has now been banned in most countries.

Adult silver Cornish rooster

U.S. Department of Agriculture photos

DUCKS are raised almost wholly for their meat. The *Muscovy* duck is a large breed of fowl, and the *Rouen* is the largest in the world. Both are common in the United States. The Muscovy was developed in Brazil and the Rouen was of French breeding stock.

Adult silver Cornish hen

GEESE are raised for their feathers and their meat. In many places they are the favorite holiday dinner. Goose down is used in the best pillows. Before metal pens came into use for writing, goose quills were in great demand. The Declaration of Independence was signed with a goose quill. The Canada goose is much smaller than most of the popular breeds.

The bronze TURKEY is the largest and most brilliantly colored. It was developed in the United States from the wild turkey of Mexico. From this same wild ancestor have come several breeds developed in Europe. The wild turkey of the eastern United States has

Wyandotte cock

Wyandotte hen

New Hampshire rooster

All photos U.S. Department of Agriculture

Day-old, cross-breed chicks

Young experimental breed turkeys

Beltsville white turkeys

also been domesticated and is called the *Narragansett.* It is a much smaller turkey than the bronze.

The term *poultry* is sometimes used to include the guinea fowl, partridge, pheasant, pigeon and quail, but most often these game birds are left out. This is especially true in the poultry industry which breeds and raises ducks and geese, turkeys, and the ever-popular chickens.

One of the major activities of the poultry industry is the raising and care of chickens for egg production. Eggs have been a vital source of protein and other nutrients since prehistoric times. Today, the egg industry is run on a highly scientific and tested basis. Poultry raisers have discovered that the number of eggs laid by a flock of chickens in one day depends on many factors. These include the amount of light within which the chickens spend the day, the amount of space each chicken has around its nesting box, daily and special diets, hereditary factors bred into each chicken, and general health. There is evidence that even air flow, humidity and temperature in the hen house affect egg laying. However, even under the widely varied conditions of small farms and country and city backyards, chickens survive and continue to lay eggs.

The raising of poultry as a source of meat is another major activity within the industry. Some birds, especially chickens, are raised for varying periods of time depending on the type of meat the market demands. Chickens to be used for roasting, for example, are usually males that are allowed to grow until they are full adult size. Broiling or frying chickens, on the other hand, are fed and treated as chicks until they are about 12 to 14 weeks old when they are sent to market.

Special breeding is carried out within the poultry industry to obtain special qualities within the birds. Breeders try to obtain chicken and turkeys with a greater proportion of white breast meat, geese with less oil in the flesh, and any fowl that will not contract the diseases that can ruin a flock of birds. J. F. B.

SEE ALSO: AGRICULTURE, BIRD, BREEDING, HEREDITY

Fox Foxes are doglike MAMMALS with bushy tails, pointed noses and ears, and short legs. They are found in many parts of the world. Two common American foxes are the gray and the red. The red fox has several color types. It may be black, silver, or a mottled mixture of red and black called a cross fox. It feeds on rodents, poultry, dead animals, and fruit.

Foxes prefer open woodlands where there is both cover and good hunting. They are solitary animals with catlike personalities. In hunting they depend on cunning and slyness. Foxes are active at night and during the early

The sly fox is a skillful hunter.

Jim Thiele: National Fish & Wildlife Service

morning and evening hours. Sometimes they are active during the day.

Dens are usually made in banks and pairs mate for the year. Litters of five to six kits are born in March or April. The female or *vixen* is fed by the male for a few days after the kits are born. Kits stay in the den for about a month and are weaned at eight weeks. Until fall, they accompany their father on hunting trips. After that they are on their own.

Arctic foxes are all white in the winter and bluish-gray in the summer. They do not hibernate but make burrows in the snow, curling up and using their tails for scarves. They put food in "deep freeze" for future use.

J. C. K.

False foxglove

Foxglove The foxglove is a plant which has tube-shaped flowers that grow along one side of a tall stem in a spike-like cluster. In Scotland, the foxglove is called "ladies' thimbles" and in Wales, "elves' gloves" or "red-fingers."

The foxglove is a PERENNIAL or BIENNIAL native to Europe and western Asia. It is a member of the figwort family. In North America it is a favorite garden flower for borders and among shrubs. Its lovely flowers range from purple, to yellow, and rose to white. The plants need little special care, liking some shade and any ordinary soil. They are propagated by seed or vegetative division.

The dried leaf of the common purple foxglove contains a powerful heart stimulant called DIGITALIS after the Latin name of the plant, *Digitalis purpurea.*

Related to the garden foxgloves are certain woodland WILD FLOWERS called *false* or wild foxglove.

J. M. C.

Fracture A fracture is a break, in this case, a break in a bone. A *simple* fracture means the bone is broken through but does not puncture the skin. A *compound* fracture punctures the skin, exposing the bone end to the outside. The bone can become infected and take a long time to heal.

In a *greenstick* fracture, the bone is cracked instead of broken completely through. These fractures heal well because they remain in good position. A fracture should be splinted so bone ends cannot move and endanger nearby tissues. Wrap the fractured part to a board or roll of cloth, or strap it to the body. Fractures must be set by a doctor within a few days.

B. M. H.

SEE ALSO: FIRST AID

Francium Francium is a radioactive element formed when ALPHA RAYS strike actinium atoms. It is an alkali metal.

Francium has atomic number 87 and its symbol is Fr. It was discovered in 1939 by Marguerite Perey at the Curie Institute in Paris. She named it in honor of France. It is the heaviest alkali metal. The atomic weight of its most stable ISOTOPE is 223. The HALF-LIFE of this isotope is only 22 minutes. Other isotopes from Fr^{217} to Fr^{224} have been identified. $Francium^{223}$ breaks down and gives off BETA RAYS and others, forming radium 223.

Besides its occurrence in Nature, francium can be produced in an alpha ray generator or an accelerator.

D. A. B.

Franck, James (1882-1964) James Franck was a German-born American atomic physicist who shared the 1925 NOBEL PRIZE in physics with GUSTAV HERTZ. They did molecular and atomic research. Franck also did research on the atomic BOMB.

Franck's research dealt with the critical energy of electrons bombarding atoms. His work supported the BOHR theory. It also involved application of the PLANCK constant. Franck did other important research in atomic and molecular physics. Later he performed extensive investigations of the biochemical processes of *photosynthesis.*

Frankincense see Forest products

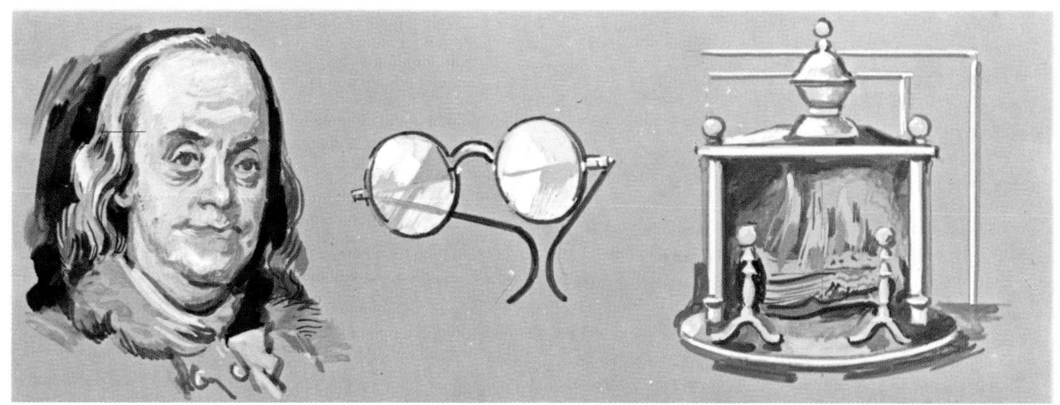

Benjamin Franklin was one of the first scientists in the United States

Franklin, Benjamin (1706-1790) Benjamin Franklin was an American scientist, inventor, statesman, businessman, philosopher, printer, author, and publisher. He was a man of many talents who had a great deal to do with the shaping of America.

Science had been an absorbing interest with Benjamin Franklin since his boyhood, but it was not until he invented the Pennsylvania fireplace, better known as the Franklin stove, in 1740 that this interest was put to practical use. The Franklin stove offered an opportunity for greatly improved heating in the colonial homes, thus creating the huge stovemaking industry in America.

In the field of electrical science, Franklin made many important contributions. He proved that LIGHTNING is electricity by flying a homemade kite in a thunderstorm. Then he invented the lightning rod to help prevent the enormous losses caused by lightning. He invented many of the terms which are still used when discussing electricity: *positive, negative, battery, conductor, armature, condenser,* etc. When his book, *Observations in Electricity,* was published in London and translated into foreign languages, Franklin became famous.

Outside of electricity, Benjamin Franklin's most important contributions to science were made in the study of the Gulf Stream and weather predictions. In 1743 he observed that storms, which appeared to come from the northeast actually moved *from* the southwest *to* the northeast. He even laid plans for the first American expedition to explore the Arctic region.

Among the many things Franklin invented were bifocal glasses, (glasses having two curves) and the platform rocker. Among the ideas he introduced to America were the use of lime to improve the soil; the manufacture of silk; the use of broom corn for brooms and whiskbrooms; and the use of yellow willow for many willow products. He also discovered that poorly ventilated rooms help spread disease.

Born on Milk Street, Boston, Massachusetts, on January 17, 1706, Benjamin was the son of Josiah Franklin, a candle and soap maker who had emigrated from Banbury, Oxfordshire, England, in 1683 with his wife Anne and their children. Anne died in 1689, and Josiah quickly remarried Abiah Folger. Benjamin was the eighth of Abiah's ten children, and the fifteenth of Josiah's seventeen. D. H. J.

Freezing point The change of state which occurs when a substance is transformed from the liquid state to the solid state is called *freezing*. The temperature at which a liquid changes to the solid state is called the *freezing point*.

The freezing point for pure water is 32°F or 0°C. When a liquid is in the process of freezing it must give up some heat to its surroundings. The heat that is given up by water when it reaches the freezing point is called the HEAT OF FUSION. This heat is given up without actually changing the temperature of the substance. The heat of fusion for water is 80 CALORIES per gram in going from 0°C liquid to 0°C ice.

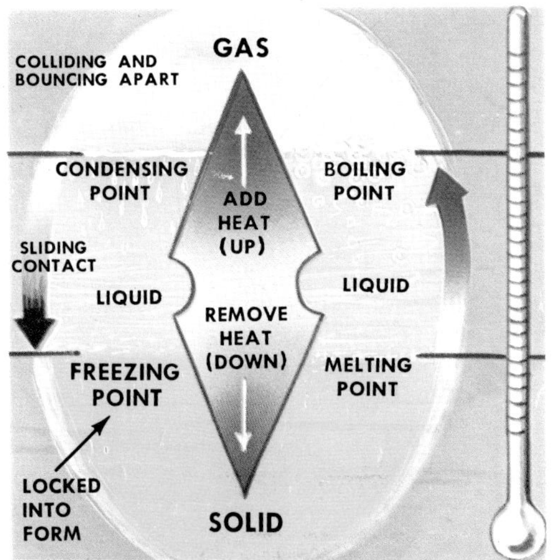

Most substances have temperatures at which a change of state occurs. The same substance may behave in three ways

Most liquids and metals contract upon freezing but water undergoes an EXPANSION. The density of ice at 0°C is only 0.91 that of water at the same temperature.

The freezing point of most substances can be raised or lowered by various means. For liquids which contract upon freezing, increased pressures will raise the freezing point. For liquids which expand, such as water, increased pressure will decrease the freezing point. Also, foreign particles such as salt crystals in solution will decrease the freezing point. Many ALLOYS of metal have a lower freezing point than the individual metals themselves. A. E. L.

SEE ALSO: SUBSTANCES, PROPERTIES OF

✳ THINGS TO DO

CAN THE FREEZING POINT OF WATER BE LOWERED BY PRESSURE?

1. **Fill a pint jar with colored water and cap it. Set the jar in a bucket of chipped ice, salt, and water. Watch the liquid carefully.** (1 pint = .5 liter)
2. **Just before it appears to reach the freezing point remove the cap. This reduces the pressure and the colored water begins to solidify immediately.**
3. **Increased pressure produces heat. Releasing the pressure removed the heat permitting the liquid to freeze.**

FREEZING (MELTING) POINTS OF COMMON SUBSTANCES*

	°C.	°F.		°C.	°F.
ALCOHOL, ETHYL (100%)	−117	−179	MERCURY	−40	−40
ALCOHOL, RUBBING (70%)	−51	−60	MOTH BALLS (P-DI-CHLOROBENZENE)	53	127
ALUMINUM	660	1220	SALT, COMMON (NaCl)	801	1481
BEEF FAT	31 to 37	88 to 98	TUNGSTEN (ELEMENT)	3390	6134
CARBON TETRA-CHLORIDE (CLEANING FLUID)	−23	−9	WATER, DISTILLED	0	32
GOLD	1063	1946			

* °C. means temperature in Centigrade degrees
°F. means temperature in Fahrenheit degrees
Minus sign (—) before number means degrees below zero

Frequency Frequency is the number of occurrences within a given period of time of some event—a cycle, vibrations, etc.—which repeats regularly. In ELECTRICITY it is the number of complete alternations per second of an alternating current.

SEE: RADIO

Freud, Sigmund (FROYD) (1856-1939) Freud was an Austrian physician. He is called the "father of psychoanalysis." He developed the method of treatment which allowed patients with nervous disorders to talk out their problems. In this way the doctor was able to help patients understand the causes of their sickness. When Dr. Freud first announced his new ideas, a storm broke in the world of MEDICINE.

Freud received his medical degree at the University of Vienna. At twenty-nine he went to Paris to study under Jean Charcot, the great neurologist. Dr. Charcot was investigating how hypnosis could be used to cure patients of nervous disorders.

Freud returned to Vienna, to find that the new theories caused an uproar. All his colleagues but Dr. Josef Breuer deserted him.

Then Dr. Freud got a startling idea. Instead of hypnotizing patients, why not keep them conscious and, with the doctor's help, have them analyze their own unconscious minds? Even Dr. Breuer could not accept this idea.

From this point Freud developed his theories of the unconscious mind and his methods of bringing repressed thoughts to the conscious mind by "free association."

At last, in 1906, recognition came to Dr. Freud. Many patients asked his help. In 1938 when Hitler invaded Austria, Dr. Freud, Jewish and also an outspoken critic of Naziism, was forced to leave Vienna and escape to London. There he continued research and headed the *International Journal of Psycho-Analysis*.

On September 23, 1939, Sigmund Freud died of cancer. D. H. J.

SEE ALSO: PSYCHOLOGY

THINGS TO DO

DOES FRICTION PRODUCE A CHARGE?

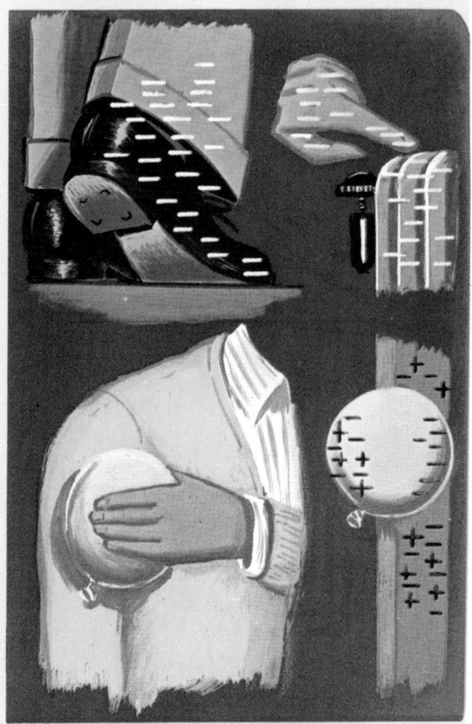

1. **On a cold, dry day shuffle your rubber-soled shoes back and forth on a wool rug. Step over to a metal pipe or radiator and quickly tap it with your finger. A spark will fly between the two objects.**
2. **Comb the fur of a cat rapidly with a rubber comb. What happens to the hair?**
3. **Blow up a balloon and tie it. Rub it on the sleeve of a woolen sweater. Touch the wall with the balloon. Will it cling to the wall?**
4. **Rub a glass rod with a silk scarf thirty times. Now hold the rod close to a small stream of water coming from a faucet. What happens to the path of the water?**
5. **Rubbing two objects together causes the electrons in the atoms of one material to jump to the other material. This upsets the neutrality of the objects and they become charged. The object that loses electrons is positively charged. The next object it meets, if neutral, will lose electrons and produce a spark.**

✳ THINGS TO DO

MEASURING THE AMOUNT OF FRICTION

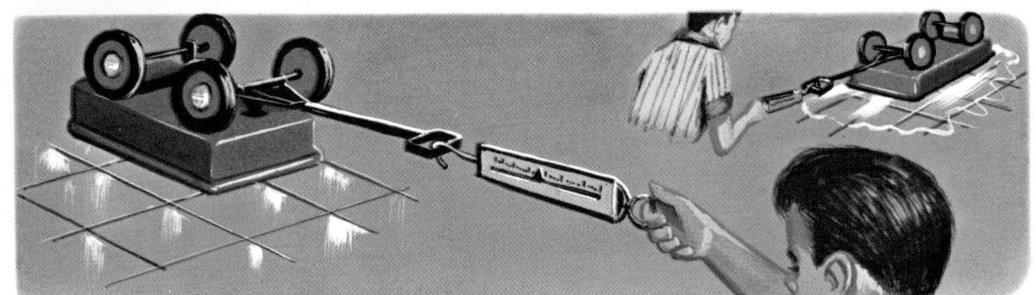

1 Turn a small wagon over on its top side. Hook the end of a spring scale in the handle and pull the wagon along the floor. How much force is necessary to move it?

2 Now put a layer of water on the floor. Repeat the experiment. Did it take less force?

3 Turn the wagon right side up on its wheels. Measure the force needed now. What does this prove?

4 The resistance between two moving objects is called friction. There is more friction between sliding objects than rolling ones. Water is a form of lubrication—makes the surfaces smoother. This cuts down on the amount of friction produced.

Friction When two bodies move while touching each other, there is a force opposing the movement known as *friction.* There are many types of friction since any moving object experiences some friction. The two main kinds of friction are *rolling* and *sliding.*

A wheel of a vehicle must constantly pull itself out of a slight depression caused by the weight of the object. The fact that the wheel is always moving up a very slight incline causes a great amount of friction. The analysis of rolling friction is quite complex. It is enough now to know that it exists.

Sliding friction, however, is represented by countless everyday experiences. Walking, nails holding boards, and stopping of a car are examples of useful sliding friction. More often than not, friction is very undesirable as in the moving parts in MACHINERY.

Since friction is a force which always acts opposite to the direction of the force moving the object, its value begins before the object actually begins to move. The force due to friction increases in value until it reaches a maximum the instant before motion actually occurs. It then drops slightly in value, remaining constant as long as the motion is unaltered. Thus it is seen that the maximum value for frictional force is obtained while the body is in the static (still) state and the kinetic (moving) value is slightly smaller. The static value is higher because the bodies settle into closer contact while at rest.

The VELOCITY of the object has very little to do with the force due to friction. The weight of the object and the condition of the two surfaces play a more important role. The amount of friction experienced by an object varies directly as the weight of the object or the force normal to the plane in which the body is moving. If the surface area of the body is increased without increasing the weight the frictional force is still the same.

These facts can be summarized into the "laws" of friction. They are: (1) within certain limits of velocity the force of kinetic friction is constant; (2) both static and kinetic friction are directly proportional to the normal force; (3) the force due to friction is independent of the contact area. The algebraic expression of these laws is

$$f = \mu N$$

where f is the force due to friction, N is the normal force and μ is called the coefficient of friction. The value of μ depends greatly on the "smoothness" of the surfaces. A. E. L.

SEE ALSO: ACCELERATION, BEARING

✳ THINGS TO DO

FROM EGG TO TADPOLE TO FROG

1 Gather a gelatinous mass of frog eggs from a pond in early spring. Place them in an aquarium.
2 Soon tiny tadpoles will wiggle out. Separate them into several containers to avoid crowding.
3 Feed the tadpoles bits of leafy vegetables and the yellow of a hard-boiled egg. Avoid overfeeding to prevent contamination of the water.
4 Observe the tadpole as it develops its legs and as the tail is absorbed.
5 Construct a semi-aquatic terrarium by placing a bowl of water in one end of an aquarium. On the other half build a land environment of sand, soil and plants.
6 As the tadpoles develop lungs they will leave the water environment and seek the land. Adult frogs like live insects for food. Do not be impatient—it may take a year or more with some species of frogs to go from egg to adult.

Frisch, Karl von (1886-1982) Frisch was an Austrian zoologist known for his studies of insect behavior and sensory physiology. He found that honeybees communicate with one another by a form of waggle dancing.

Frisch first studied the habits of honeybees, and then devised experiments to test their responses to different situations. It was through such observations that he discovered how honeybee workers communicate the location of a food source. Through experimentation he was able to train bees and observe the manner in which they communicate information to the other worker bees.

For this work he received the NOBEL PRIZE in medicine and physiology in 1973 with KONRAD LORENZ and NICKOLAAS TINBERGEN.

P.P.S.

SEE ALSO: BEES

The bullfrog, a large frog, is hunted for food
Courtesy Society For Visual Education, Inc.

Frog Frogs are AMPHIBIANS. They have smooth, moist skins, webbed feet, and live in water or damp places. They are called amphibians because many of them have a gilled water-living tadpole or larval stage. Later these tadpoles change or metamorphose into land-living adults. Some frogs lay their eggs on land. In these the tadpoles metamorphose inside the egg. Others lay eggs near a pond in a frothy mass of jelly with a liquid center. Tadpoles live in the liquid until washed, by rain, into the pond. Out of 3,000 species of amphibians, 2,700 of the species are frogs and toads.

Frogs, as amphibians, are members of a group that are transitional or in between aquatic fish and terrestrial or land-living reptiles. Aquatic reproduction and smooth moist skins limit them to habitats that are damp or near water. However, many of their characteristics are adaptations for living upon land.

Frogs have legs rather than fins. They are agile and expert jumpers. With jumping legs instead of fins, limb muscles are better developed. The vertebral column has become adapted to withstand the jars associated with jumping.

Breathing in tadpoles is by gills. Oxygen is taken in through them into the bloodstream. Adult frogs develop lungs like reptiles and other terrestrial animals. The lungs are simple sacs. Some oxygen enters the bloodstream through the lungs, but most breathing takes place through the skin. The transition to lung breathing is not complete.

When lungs develop, in order for them to become efficient, the circulatory system must develop two circuits, one between the heart and body, and one between the heart and lungs. A four-chambered heart develops. The right side handles deoxygenated blood, receiving it from the body and sending it to the lungs. The left side handles oxygenated blood, receiving it from the lungs and sending it to the body. In the frog the system is not perfected. The heart is three-chambered. It has two auricles for receiving blood from body and lungs. The ventricle still has a single chamber in which both types of blood mix. Skin breathing makes up the oxygen deficit.

J. C. K.

SEE ALSO: AMPHIBIANS, METAMORPHOSIS

Frond see Fern

Front see Air masses, Cyclone, Weather, Weather forecasting

Frontal lobe see Brain

Frost Sometimes air is cooled to a temperature where it can no longer hold all the moisture or water it contains. When this happens, the air is said to have reached the *dew point*. The water will condense on the surroundings which are cooler than the air itself.

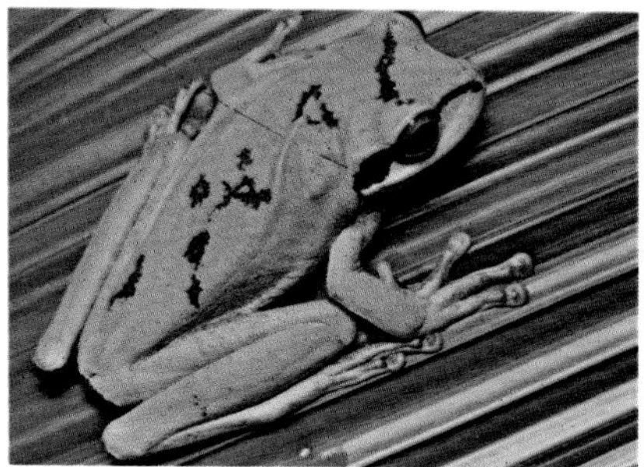

Buchsbaum

Tree frogs have odd feet useful for climbing

Sometimes this condensation is frost. If the temperature of the object on which the water condenses is above the freezing point of water, the condensation is observed as dew. If, however, the temperature of the object is below the freezing point, the water vapor forms ice crystals and the condensation is observed as frost.

A. E. L.

✳ THINGS TO DO

WHAT IS A FROZEN DEW DROP?

1. **Remove the paper jacket from a tin food can. Fill the can with two cups of broken ice cubes. Add one-half cup of table or rock salt.**
2. **Stir the mixture vigorously, then let it stand for half an hour.**
3. **When the moisture in the warm air surrounding the can is cooled it condenses on the outside of the can. These are dew drops. Soon they will freeze, forming frost.**

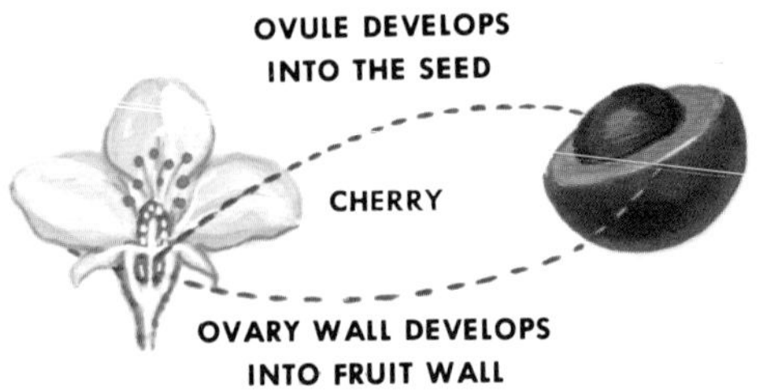

BLACKBERRY

BLUEBERRY

Frostbite Frostbite is a common type of injury from extreme cold, usually affecting the ears, nose, fingers or toes. At first the frostbitten part feels cold and stings. It is alternately red and white. Then it becomes numb, and finally loses all feeling and remains white.

When the frostbitten part is warmed, it becomes red or blue, painful and swollen. Sometimes blisters form, and the skin peels. In severe cases, some parts die, and must be removed by SURGERY.

If a part becomes frostbitten, it should not be exercised or massaged, nor should it be rubbed with snow. It should be soaked in warm (100° F or 37.8° C) water until it reaches room temperature. J.K.L.

Fruit It is an organ of flowering plants. A fruit is one or more ripe or mature ovaries of a FLOWER. Joined ovaries of many flowers also form a single fruit. Sometimes a fruit includes other flower parts. A fruit usually has one or more seeds. Some develop without seeds.

Fruit are classified as fleshy or dry. This refers to the wall which houses ripe ovules or seeds. The fruit wall is called *pericarp*. The outer layer is *exocarp,* the middle is *mesocarp,* followed by the inside layer of *endocarp*. Nuts have a dry wall, while berries are all fleshy.

Fruit production is limited to ANGIOSPERMS, the only class of plants with flowers. Following POLLINATION and FERTILIZATION, changes begin to occur within the flower which cause a fruit to form. Flower parts not involved in a particular fruit wither up and drop off. Annual plants die soon after fruit and seeds are produced.

Fruits vary in color from white to almost black. *Anthocyanins* are pigments dissolved in cell sap. They appear late in the development and give the red color to ripe apples and yellow to ripe pears.

DRY FRUITS

The wall or pericarp of many ripe fruits is dry. Their colors are usually gray, brown, or some other dull shade. Seeds, rather than the pericarp, contain the food. They are simple fruits which develop generally from a single ovary. Dry fruits are of two kinds—*indehiscent* and *dehiscent*.

Indehiscent fruits do not split open or disperse seeds when they reach maturity. They are easily stored for they have no fleshy part to decay. Such fruits as GRAINS and NUTS may not disintegrate for years. Indehiscent fruits are grouped in the following categories: achene, samara, nut, caryopsis, schizocarp, and anthocarp.

Achene This fruit develops from an ovary with one carpel. The single small seed is attached to the fruit wall at one spot but can be easily separated from it. This wall is so thin that its fruit is often called a "seed." Sometimes the calyx remains attached to the ovary and the fruit ends up with long hairs, thin scales, spines, or hooked bristles. These structures aid in seed dispersal. Achene fruits are found on sunflower, dandelion, beggartick, buckwheat, and the individual "seeds" or fruits on the strawberry.

Samara This dry fruit has one or two seeds. Part of the ovary wall grows out at maturity to form papery wings. Such fruit may be carried by wind currents for great distances. Samara fruit appears on maple, ash, elm, box elder, tree-of-heaven, and birch trees.

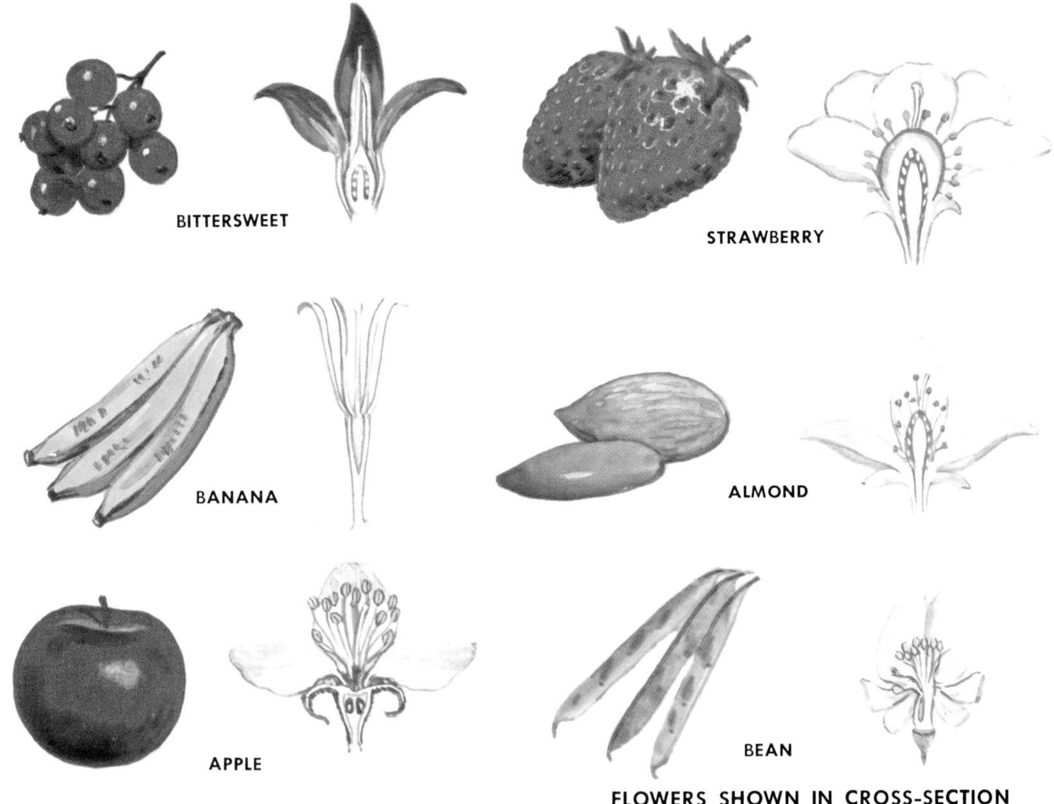

The main parts of fruit correspond to parts of the flower from which they grow

Nut This is a botanical classification that does not include many fruits commonly called nuts. Part or all of the fruit wall is woody or stony. This shell is often covered with a fibrous, scaly, or hairy coat produced by flower parts other than the ovary. Usually one seed develops in an ovary of more than one carpel. True nuts are grown on oak, hickory, chestnut, and beechnut trees. Individual fruits of some multiples, as in mulberry, are called nutlets.

Caryopsis Grain is the common name for this group. The single pistil, composed of three carpels, matures into a one-seeded fruit. The wall is so tightly attached to the seed that it takes a special process in milling to remove it. Members of the grass family all produce this type of dry indehiscent fruit.

Schizocarp Carrot, parsnip, and celery are examples of plants bearing this fruit. Two carpels in the ovary separate and each half develops into an individual fruit. The single seed fills the whole chamber and is often closely attached to the fruit wall.

Anthocarp When the ovary and part of the surrounding perianth develop into a dry fruit it is called an anthocarp. Members of the four-o'clock family, such as verbena and bougainvillea, have fruit walls composed, in part, of the base of the calyx.

Dehiscent fruits split open or disperse seeds when they reach maturity. They are simple fruits which develop from a single ovary. The pericarp is often a drab color and forms into a variety of shapes. It usually remains on the plant after seeds are dispersed. Dehiscent fruits are grouped in the following categories: capsule, follicle, legume, and silique.

Capsule It develops from a compound ovary. Each carpel contains several or many seeds. When the fruit ripens each carpel opens lengthwise, splitting along three or more seams. Some capsules have pores or a transverse lid at the top. Wind blowing the plant shakes out seeds. Capsule fruits are found on cotton, poppy, pigweed, and iris.

Follicle This fruit splits along one side or suture. It develops from one ovary with one carpel. When fruit is ripe, the wind shaking it or a bump by an animal will disperse seeds. Larkspur, magnolia, and Christmas rose bear follicle fruit.

Legume If the mature ovary wall dehisces or splits along two seams, it is a legume or pod. A single carpel holds one to many seeds. As fruit dries, it often squirts or pops out seeds. A few plants with pods, such as the peanut, bur clover, and alfalfa, do not dehisce. Peas, wisteria, and vetch are legumes.

Silique Mustard, cabbage, and rutabaga have this fruit classification. The superior ovary has four carpels. The outer two are sterile while the inner two produce seeds. The latter dehisces when fruit matures.

FLESHY FRUITS

Part or all of the wall of many ripe fruits is fleshy. It may develop from a single ovary of a single flower, many ovaries of a single flower, or from many ovaries of many flowers joined together. Some part of the pericarp may be stony, papery, or leathery. Flesh of some fruits develops from other parts of the flower as well as the ovary. Fleshy fruits are grouped into the following divisions: berry, drupe, pome or accessory, aggregate, and multiple.

Berry When the entire wall of a compound ovary becomes fleshy at maturity the fruit is a berry. It may contain one or many seeds. Blueberry, currant, and tomato are true berries. Pepo is a type of berry. The rind and receptacle form the exocarp. Pulp is mesocarp and endocarp. Melons are pepos. Hesperidium is another berry variety. The rind is the outer and middle layers, while pulp is endocarp. Citrus fruits are of this kind. Individual fruits of certain multiples, as in pineapple, are berries.

Drupe This is any fruit which forms a hard, stony endocarp or pit. It begins from a one-carpelled ovary and produces one seed. The pit is made of stone cells. Olive, peach, and avocado are drupes. Fleshy pericarp of almond and coconut becomes dry and forms the *hull* or outer covering. Individual fruits on a raspberry and blackberry are drupes.

Pome or *accessory* Flesh of this fruit develops from the receptacle and/or other parts of the floral tube, as well as the ovary wall. Only the core of the pear is an ovary, the remainder being swollen ends of petals and other parts. Apple and quince are pomes. Fleshy sepals are composed mostly of mulberry, a multiple fruit. The upper end of the flower stalk forms much of the fleshiness in the aggregate fruit of the strawberry.

Aggregate This fruit forms from many individual ovaries of a single flower attached to one receptacle. It is really a group of simple fruits grown together and is often classified as one of those previously described. Blackberry, raspberry, and rose hips are aggregate types.

Multiple This fruit forms from many ovaries of many flowers joined together. In some cases even the receptacle may be part of the fleshy wall. This, too, is often classified as one of those previously described. Pineapple is composed of many berries on a fleshy stem. Fig and mulberry are examples of other multiples.

H. J. C.

SEE ALSO: CITRUS FRUITS, HORTICULTURE, HYBRIDIZATION, PARTHENOCARPY

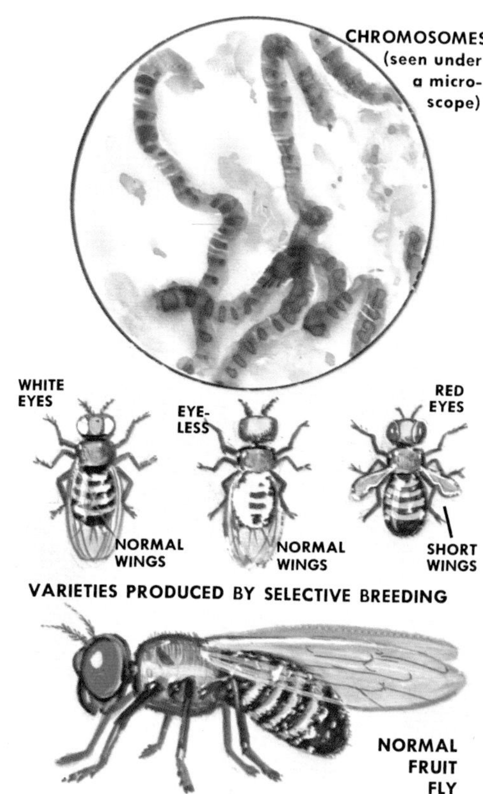

Fruit fly There are three families of flies called fruit flies. Usually both adults and young feed upon various kinds of fruit. Of all these small INSECTS, the vinegar, or red-eyed pomace fly, is the best known. Geneticists, beginning with Dr. T. H. Morgan, have spent years studying the inheritance of them. Bodies are grayish with dark-brown stripes or a short, wide abdomen. Thorax and abdominal tips are also brown. Wings are few-veined, broad, and transparent. In nature, the eyes are usually red. Males have a sex comb on their forelegs.

Vinegar flies are excellent for breeding experiments. They are small and will live and reproduce in a small milk bottle containing

✳ **THINGS TO DO**

WILL FRUIT FLY PARENTS WITH RED EYES PRODUCE RED-EYED OFFSPRING ?

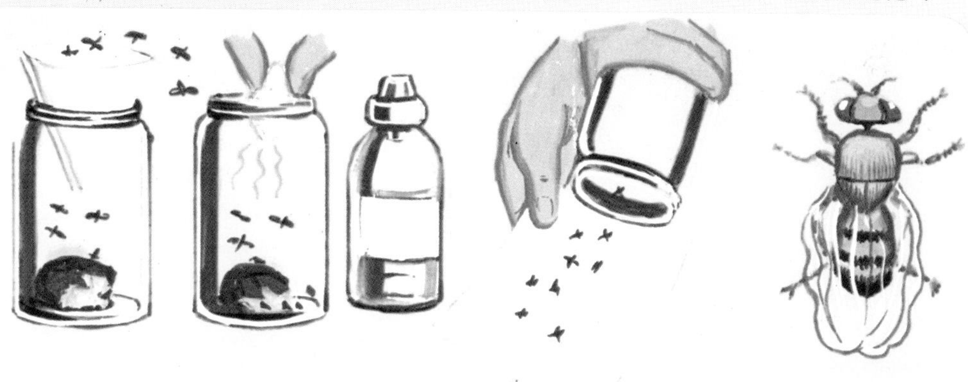

1 **Cut a piece of decayed apple or banana and place it into a glass jar. Put in a crumpled paper towel.**

2 **Place a plastic or paper funnel in mouth of the jar. After several fruit flies have been captured in the jar remove the funnel and cover the jar opening with a cloth. These flies seem to appear wherever fruit is decaying.**

3 **It takes about two weeks for the life cycle of the fruit fly. The adults lay eggs, the eggs develop into larva, and the larva mature into adults. The male has a darker band on the end of his abdomen.**

4 **In order to observe the sexes and to separate them into pairs it is necessary to put them to sleep for awhile. Use a small wad of cotton saturated with carbon tetrachloride. DO NOT BREATHE THIS CHEMICAL. Hold it in the jar only a few seconds.**

5 **The flies may be poured out on to a white sheet of paper. With a hand lens pick a male and a female for each new culture. Write down the characteristics of each pair.**

6 **Breed each pair in a separate jar, prepared as in the original jar. Observe and record each generation. Will two red-eyed parents always produce red-eyed offspring?**

mashed banana. They have short life cycles. At room temperature, the egg period is about 2 days, the larval about 6, and the pupal about 5 days. Thus the entire cycle of complete METAMORPHOSIS takes place in less than two weeks. Twenty generations a year can be raised. Another advantage these flies have for experimental use is the small number of CHROMOSOMES present in their cells. With only one small and three large pairs, any changes in structure are readily observed.

The inheritance of such characteristics as eye color, body color, wing length, and body bristle length were studied. Occasionally, a few flies of abnormal appearance were discovered among the cultures. These changed characteristics were always inherited, showing that the GENE for that characteristic had changed. Such genic changes were called MUTATIONS, and the flies with them mutants. Changes in eye color and shape and wing length are examples of the mutations obtained. X raying flies increased the rate of mutation.

Genes for red and white eyes were found to be located on a pair of chromosomes which were not alike in the male but were in the female. These were called the sex chromosomes. X-rayed flies, in which the complete set of chromosomes was doubled, halved, or tripled, showed that the other chromosomes had a role in sex determination also, since both intersexes and super males and females were produced with normal sets of sex chromosomes. J. C. K.

SEE ALSO: GENETICS, HEREDITY, MENDEL

FSH (follicle stimulating hormone) see Estrous cycle, Menstruation

Fuchsia flowers have four slender curved petals

Fuchsia (FEW-shuh) The drooping FLOWER is purple, red, or white. It is pollinated by birds. The FRUIT develops into a fleshy berry.

The simple, serrated LEAVES have pinnate venation and are opposite on the stem. The flower is perfect with 8 stamens and 1 pistil with 4 carpels. There are about 60 species belonging to the family Onagraceae. H. J. C.

Fucus (FEW-kuss) Fucus is a widely-distributed kind of alga found in colder waters. It is common along sea coasts. A branched, leathery rockweed held fast by disks, fucus grows from several inches (centimeters) to over a foot (.3 meter) in length. Growth occurs at the tip of each branch.

Characterized by the brown pigment *fucoxanthin,* which masks the chlorophyll, fucus belongs to the *Phaeophyta* group. All but three of the nine hundred species of this group are marine.

Fucus differs from other brown alga in that the ZYGOTE, formed by the union of the male and female gametes directly, develops into another sexual plant which produces male and female gametes. In many ALGAE, a sexual plant generation (producing gametes with half the number of chromosomes) alternates with an asexual plant (gametes having full number of chromosomes.) E.M.S.

SEE ALSO: ALTERNATION OF GENERATIONS, MARINE BIOLOGY, SPORE FORMATION

Fucus, alga of ocean shores

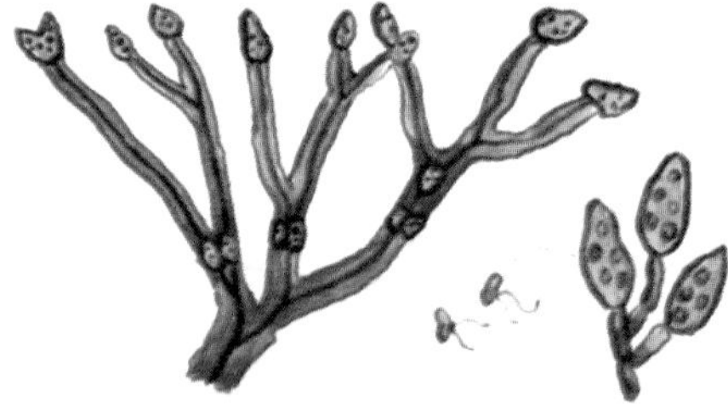

Fuel Fuel is a substance or radiant source from which heat or the ENERGY to do work can be obtained. The most popular fuels in the world today are wood, coal, petroleum, and natural gas. Two alternatives—sunlight and *fissionable* elements (such as uranium and plutonium)—are growing in importance and may one day replace other fuels. Even hydrogen, one of the constituents of water, can become a fuel when harnessed in *fusion reactions*—the power source of stars.

To unleash the energy stored within it, a fuel must be converted from its original form. Food is a fuel. Its chemical energy enables the human body and the bodies of other animals to perform work. Most fuels are used to generate heat. Various processes convert fuels to heat through *exothermic reactions. Heat energy* created by the burning, or combustion, of fossil fuels such as coal, petroleum, and natural gas can be used to produce the steam that drives large turbines and locomotives. The *chemical energy* in gasoline is released by exothermic reactions to power engines, such as those that drive automobiles. Uranium, a nuclear fuel, unleashes its energy through an entirely different process—the splitting of atomic nuclei. Even sunlight—*solar energy*—can be harnessed to do work when the sun's rays are transformed by a solar collector into heat, electricity, or the *photochemical energy* used to power many chemical reactions. Green plants are nature's best solar collectors. Through use of their green *chlorophyll,* plants collect the sun's radiant energy to produce the chemical reactions that manufacture a plant's food. This process is called PHOTOSYNTHESIS.

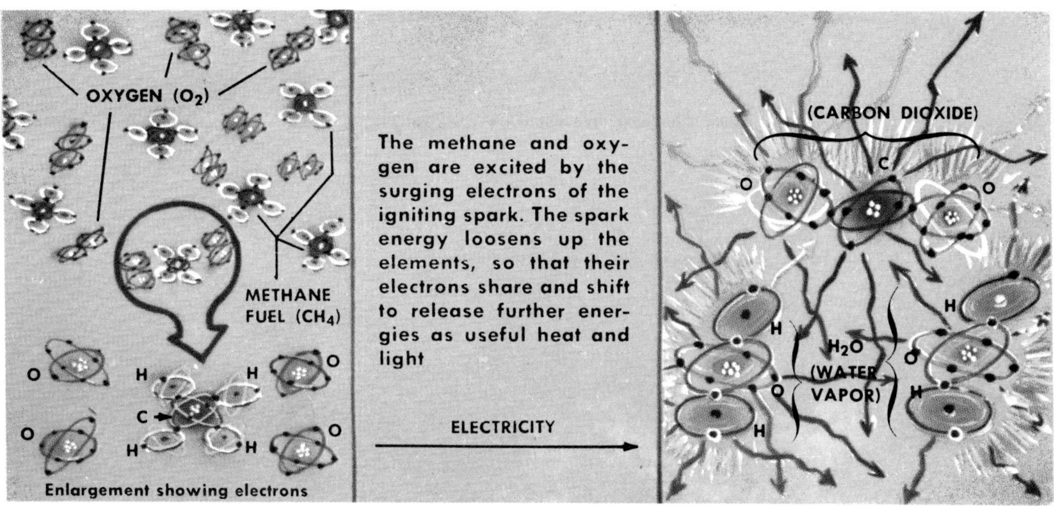

Chemical reaction (burning) of a high-energy chemical fuel releases useful energy

COMBUSTION

Combustion, or burning, frees the energy in many *carbon-based fuels* such as wood, oil, coal, gasoline, and natural gas. When sufficiently heated in the presence of oxygen, components in these fuels will combine with the oxygen. The primary end products of fuel combustion are carbon dioxide, water, and heat. There are other end products, some of which—called *pollutants*—are harmful to the environment.

Coal is a naturally abundant fuel source. In recent years, however, its use has been declining, primarily because of public concern over the pollution created when coal is burned. Cleaning up coal-combustion gases before they are released into the environment is very costly.

There are three major types of pollutants produced by the combustion of carbon-based fuels—sulfur oxides, nitrous oxides, and carbon dioxide. The sulfurous and nitrous oxides have been shown to cause health problems in humans, to decrease visibility in the air, to kill aquatic life in many lakes, and even to eat away at many building materials, such as marble.

NUCLEAR FUEL

Nuclear fuel is an especially rich source of energy. One pound (0.45 kilogram) of uranium, for example, produces as much heat through fission reactions as would be produced by burning 3,000,000 pounds (1,360,776 kilograms) of coal. Nuclear power plants in operation today produce their heat energy—by fission, the splitting of atomic nuclei.

In nuclear fusion, the nuclei of lightweight atoms join, or fuse, to form a heavier and more tightly bound nucleus. The enormous energy created in the sun and other stars is believed to occur through fusion reactions. The energy created from a single fusion reaction is less than that produced by the fissioning of a single atom. However, the nuclear fuels involved in each process are quite different. The atoms used in fusion—normally heavy forms of hydrogen—have an atomic weight close to 1. Each atom of the uranium fuel used in fission has an atomic weight of slightly more than 238. Therefore, when comparing the energy produced against the mass of the atoms each process involves, it turns out that fusion reactions create amounts of energy similar to or even greater than is created in a single fission reaction.

In a nuclear engine such as below, uranium-235 fuel (the internal black rods) generates heat by radioactive disintegration. This heat energy boils water (red) which makes steam. The steam runs a steam turbine which produces power to accomplish some kind of work

Civil Air Patrol

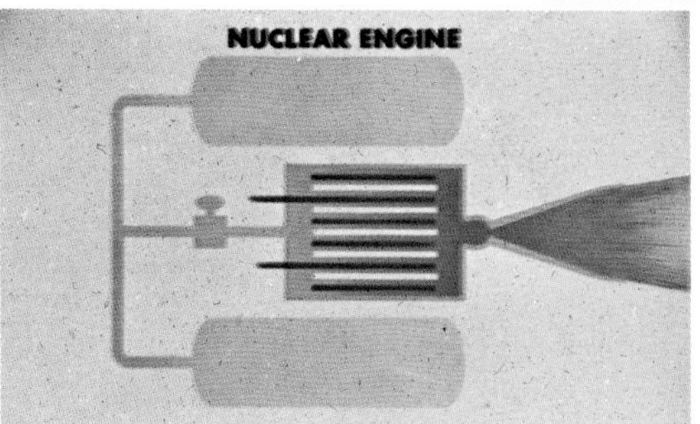

SOLAR ENERGY

Sunlight remains largely untapped as a source of energy. Since the energy crisis of the 1970s, however, research to develop ways to use the sun's energy has expanded.

Photovoltaic solar cells convert sunlight directly into electrical energy. Though still very costly and largely inefficient (the best cells were only about 10 percent efficient in 1982), solar-generated power provides for all electrical needs in many experimental homes and businesses.

Solar collectors use a blackened coating over an absorber device to collect heat. Water or air flowing through the absorber carries heat from the collector to a heat-storage device for later use.

Solar concentrators use mirrors or lenses to focus incoming sunlight into very intense heat sources. Temperatures of more than

The energy of the sun can be collected. The heat from the sun is concentrated and stored. This heat is then used to generate steam which produces mechanical power.

600° F. (316° C.) can be achieved with very efficient concentrators. Most solar concentrators are being developed to replace combustion fuels as a way of creating high-temperature steam for industrial processes.

Solar ponds are large pools of water that collect sunlight's heat energy in the form of hot water. Large solar ponds provide year-round hot water for industry and agriculture, even in snowy climates.

FUEL CELL

A fuel cell is a device (still largely experimental) that converts chemical energy into a direct electric current. Car batteries might be classified as fuel cells, except that they use expensive fuels such as lead and zinc. A true fuel cell should use a basic fuel, such as

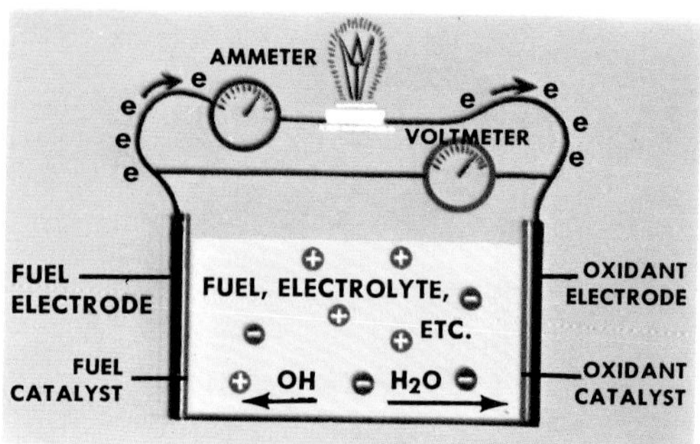

The energy in a fuel cell goes directly from chemical to electrical. Because it bypasses the intermediate steps, a fuel cell has an efficiency of almost twice that of the most advanced steam turbines

coal, oil, or natural gas, and should operate with an efficiency of close to 75 percent. This means it should be able to transform 75 percent of its fuel's chemical energy into electrical energy. Even the steam turbine, the most efficient method of producing electricity today, is only 40 percent efficient. J.R.S.

SEE ALSO: COMBUSTION, ENERGY, ENGINES, HEAT, NUCLEAR SCIENCE, ROCKET PROPELLANTS

Fuel cell see Battery, Electrochemistry, Electrolysis, Fuel

Fulcrum see Machines, simple; Torque

Fuller's earth Fuller's earth is composed mainly of CLAY with some silicates. It is used to remove the oils from raw wool and is an important agent in oil refining.

Fulton, Robert (1765-1815) Robert Fulton was an American engineer who invented the first successful steamboat. He also gained fame as the designer of canal locks that used inclined planes and as the author of a book on the improvement of canal travel. A man of many interests, he invented machines for spinning flax, for making ropes, and for sawing and polishing marble.

Robert Fulton was born in Little Britain, Pennsylvania, now named Fulton in his honor. At a very early age he was apprenticed to a jeweler in Philadelphia, but he later used his artistic ability to do portrait and landscape painting. When he was twenty-two years old he went to England to study, and there he became extremely interested in engineering. After he had designed the canal locks and written his book on canal navigation, he traveled to Paris where he built a submarine called the *Nautilus*. It was at this time that he built a ship operated by steam.

Returning to the United States, he and Robert Livingston constructed the steamship *Clermont* which traveled between New York and Albany on the Hudson River. Then in 1814 Fulton constructed for the government the first steam warship. He named this ship the *Fulton*. D. H. J.

Fumarole Fumaroles are holes or fissures in the ground from which steam and other gases escape. They are associated with volcanic activity. Many are found in the Valley of Ten Thousand Smokes in Alaska.

Fumigant A fumigant is a gas or a vapor that is used to kill insects, vermin, mice and other rodents, and disease germs. Fumigants are poisonous to breathe and are used in tightly sealed rooms, warehouses, mills, grain bins, and any other places that need to be disinfected.

Hydrocyanic gas is the most common fumigant gas. It will kill anything that requires oxygen to live and is quickly fatal to humans. It is a powerful and penetrating gas with a bitter-almond odor. Because of its danger, hydrogen cyanide is usually used in ships, mills, factories, warehouses and other places that can be tightly sealed.

Sulfur dioxide, chlorine gas, FORMALDEHYDE, and chloropicrin are used to kill disease germs. They are all fatal but have an odor to warn of their presence. Formaldehyde and chloropicrin are probably the best of the four. Chlorine gas is not always trustworthy, and sulfur dioxide tarnishes metal and ruins fabrics when it comes in contact with them. A fumigant with a CARBON TETRACHLORIDE base is commonly used to protect bulk grains. J. D. B.

SEE ALSO: ANTISEPTICS, INSECTICIDES

Fungicides (FUN-juh-sides) Poisons that are used to kill or slow down the growth of fungi are called fungicides. These chemicals are put on infected plants by spraying or dusting. They are applied several days apart as the fungus spores arrive. People use fungicides on such diseases as apple scab, powdery mildew, corn smut, and wheat rust.

The early chemicals were *inorganic*. They contained copper, zinc, mercury, or sulfur. Currently, more fungicides are *organic* compounds. If the infection is too advanced, the fungicide is ineffective. Therefore, seeds are often coated with fungicides before planting. Vulnerable young seedlings are protected by using a solution of fungicide to water the soil. In large agricultural areas airplanes are employed to dust or spray crops.

A new technique called chemotherapy requires injection of an antibiotic, such as cycloheximide or griseofulvin. It is absorbed by a plant and carried through the vascular system to the infected areas. This method is used on elm trees that have been exposed to the Dutch elm fungus. H.J.C.

Fungus It is a simple plant which cannot make carbohydrates. It does not have the green pigment or chlorophyll. Fungi must get their food from other living things or from dead material. They lack true roots, stems, and leaves. The body of these plants may be a single cell, a mass of cells, or long threads or filaments. Cell walls are made of chitin, but some may be of cellulose.

The vegetative form of most fungi is a filament or *hyphae*. It may be single or multicellular. A mass of hyphae is called the *mycelium*. Absorbing hyphae or haustoria can enter living cells to get nourishment. Rhizoids are hyphae which anchor the plant to its host. Fungi are parasitic or saprophytic.

Plants without true leaves, stems, or roots are grouped as *thallophytes* (from the Greek *thallus* or shoot and *phyte* or plant). Thallophytes with chlorophyll are classified as

ALGAE; those without chlorophyll are classed as fungi. The name *fungi* popularly includes three distinct groups: BACTERIA, slime molds, and true fungi. True fungi include toadstools, yeast, puffballs, mushrooms, mildews, rusts, and smuts.

Structure of a true fungus

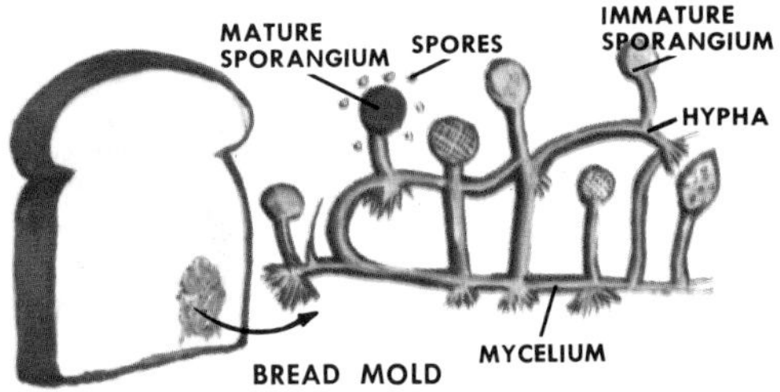

A tree fungus (below, left)

Courtesy Society For Visual Education, Inc.

A fungus has penetrated deep into the tissues of this apple

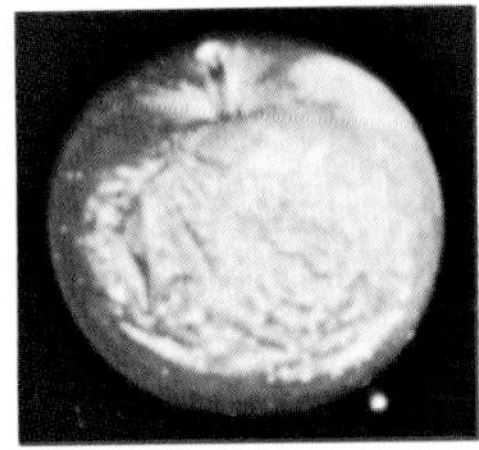

They secrete enzymes which digest food outside their cell walls. This is absorbed for use by the fungus cells.

The reproductive forms of most fungi are of two kinds. Asexually they reproduce by simple cell division, fragmentation, or spore formation. Sexually they produce spore-bearing hyphae called *sporophores*. The antheridium is the male hyphae and the oogonium the female one. A union of sex cells produces a zygote.

Algae-like Fungi (Class Phycomycetes)

These plants are one-celled or possess hyphae with no internal or cross walls. Those living in the water have zoospores, which are motile. The land and epiphyte kinds have immotile spores. There are about 1,200 species including bread MOLD, downy MILDEW, potato BLIGHT, and crown wart on alfalfa.

Sac Fungi (Class Ascomycetes)

This group may be single-celled or multicellular with cross walls. The one common characteristic is the possession of a saclike sporangium or ascus which produces eight spores. There are around 40,000 species including YEAST, penicillium, MOREL, truffle, ergot, powdery mildew, leaf curl, and blight.

Club Fungi (Class Basidiomycetes)

All members of this class have a structure on the end of a hypha which produces four external spores. They have no specialized sex organs but all reproduce sexually. Some are heterothallic, others homothallic. There are about 15,000 species including MUSHROOM, TOADSTOOL, puffball, smut, stinkhorn, tree bracket, and RUST.

Imperfect Fungi (Class Deuteromycetes)

The classification is artificial in this class. They are clumped together because no sexual structure has been found as yet. They possess sterile mycelium and reproduce only asexually. The many species include fungi which cause lung disease, RINGWORM, barber's itch, and numerous plant diseases.

Slime Fungi (Class Myxomycetes)

These living things are not true fungi. They may be plants because their spores have cellulose walls. They could be animals for they creep over dead logs and leaves in an amoeboid fashion. Their naked protoplasm has many nuclei and no cross walls. All are saprophytic.

Fungi belong to the division Eumycophyta under the subkingdom THALLOPHYTA.

H. J. C.

SEE ALSO: ECONOMIC BOTANY; PLANTS, CLASSIFICATION OF; SPORE FORMATION

Fur Fur is the hair covering of a wild or domestic mammal. A mammal's body has two types of fur. The longer, outer fur sheds water and is called *guard hair*. The inner hair is shorter and softer. This inner hair keeps the animal warm because it acts as insulation, its tiny hair fibers preventing the escape of body heat. In warm weather, when the animal no longer needs as much inner fur, some of it may be shed.

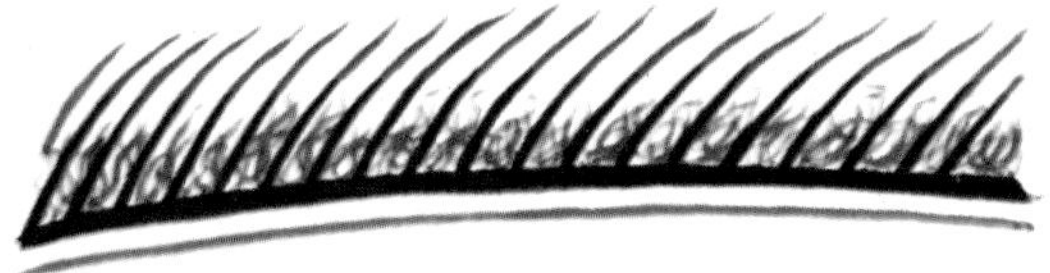

Cross-section of fur, showing guard hairs and inner hairs

Furnace A furnace is a structure or chamber in which a very hot fire can be generated. It both provides an enclosure for firing equipment and isolates and controls the fire.

SEE: HEAT

Fuse A fuse is a safety device that helps prevent fires due to electrical wires that get too hot. Part of an electric circuit, the fuse allows ELECTRICITY to flow through it. However, built into the fuse is a strip of metal that melts at a relatively low temperature. If the wires are carrying more electric current than they are designed to carry, the strip of metal will melt, or the fuse will blow, and the electric circuit will be broken.

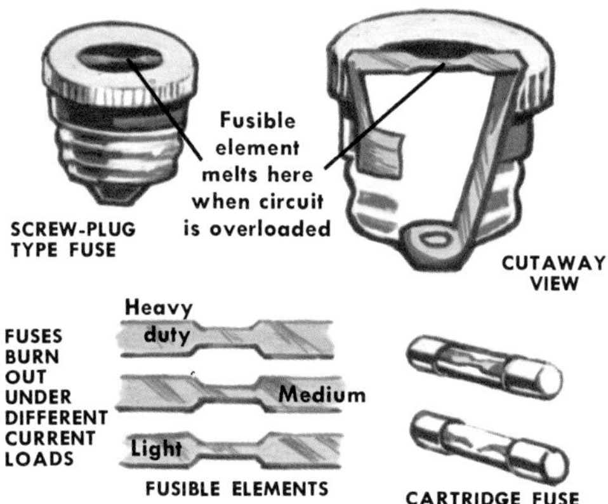

There are two kinds of fuses. One, a *plug* fuse, looks much like the socket of a light bulb and screws into the circuit. The other, a *cartridge* fuse, is long and narrow.

When a fuse is blown it must be replaced before electric current can again flow. Occasionally someone will replace a plug fuse with a copper penny. This is very dangerous, because the penny does not melt at low temperatures and will not break the electric circuit when the wires become too hot. Because fuses must be replaced, many people are now using circuit breakers. They break the flow when the wires become hot and can be reset after the fault in the circuit is corrected. J. D. B.

Fusion see Nuclear science glossary

✳ THINGS TO DO

HOW DOES A FUSE BREAK A CIRCUIT?

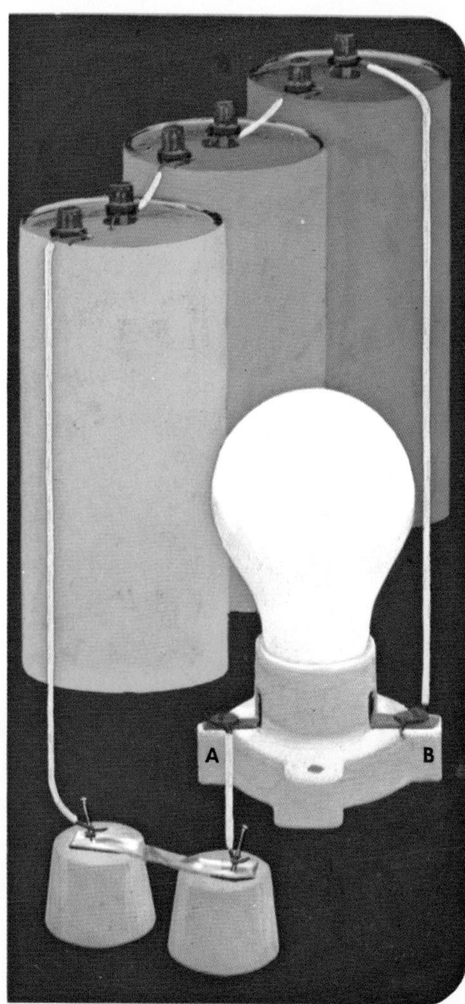

1. **Connect three dry cells in series with cut lengths of bell wire.**
2. **Cut a strip of thin metal foil, ⅛″ wide, to serve as the fuse.** ⅛″ = 3.18 mm.
3. **Insert a pin through each end of the strip. Stick the pins with the strip into the tops of two corks.**
4. **With a piece of wire, connect the first dry cell to one pin. Connect the wire from the third cell to post A on a light socket. Run a wire from post B on the socket to the second pin.**
5. **With light burning, take another wire and short the circuit by touching one end to A and the other to B. Heat will melt the foil fuse and break the connection. What happens to the light?**

G The letter g is used to tell how much acceleration is being applied to an object. The acceleration due to gravity is assumed to be one g. When an acceleration of 2 g's is exerted on a person weighing 125 pounds (56.7 kilograms) he is experiencing a weight equal to 250 pounds (113.4 kilograms). Zero g is the condition of weightlessness experienced by astronauts.

Pilots must withstand several g's when they are pulling out of a dive. An acceleration of 5 g's may cause a person to gray out for a few seconds. J. D. B.

SEE ALSO: ASTRONAUT, SPACE TRAVEL, WEIGHTLESSNESS

Gabbro see Rocks

Gabor, Dennis (1900-1979) Dennis Gabor is credited with inventing the HOLOGRAM (a three-dimensional picture). For this he received the NOBEL PRIZE in physics in 1971.

A Hungarian, Gabor settled in England in 1933. He became an industrial scientist and invented holography while working on improvements for the electron microscope. During his career he patented more than 100 inventions. A.J.H.

Gadolinium (gad-uh-LINN-ee-um) Gadolinium is ELEMENT number 64. It was discovered in 1886 by J. de Marignac. Gadolinium is a silver-white METAL. As with many of the rare earths, it is strongly paramagnetic. It is found in combination with *gadolinite* and certain other minerals.

Gadolinium is a member of the lanthanide, RARE-EARTH series. This series resembles more common substances, such as lime and magnesia, which were once known as *earths.* Gadolinium (symbol Gd) has an atomic weight of 157.25. It has seven stable ISOTOPES, two of which, Gd_{155} and Gd_{157}, can capture neutrons in a nuclear fission reaction, making it useful in controlling or destroying nuclear chain reactions.

SEE ALSO: ATOM, ELEMENTS J.R.S.

Gaillardia (gay-LAR-dee-uh) The gaillardia is a member of the composite family of flowering plants. The ray flowers are yellow, and the center disk flowers are red to purple. The plant will bloom almost all summer.

Gaillardias may be annuals, biennials, or perennials. Propagation is done by cuttings as well as by seeds. The plants need full sun and well-drained, slightly acid (*p*H 6.0 to 7.0) soil. Seeds take about two weeks to germinate. Since the stems are over 2 feet (.61 meter) long, gaillardias are usually planted toward the back of a flower border. H.J.C.

SEE ALSO: COMPOSITE FLOWER

Gajdusek, Daniel Carleton (1923-) He and Dr. Baruch Samuel Blumberg were jointly awarded the 1976 NOBEL PRIZE in medicine for their discoveries concerning new mechanisms for the origin and spreading of infectious diseases.

Dr. Gajdusek studied the transmission of viruses related to *neurological* disorders. His research was conducted while serving as a staff member at the National Institutes of Health's Institute of Neurological Diseases and Stroke. His other research interests include protein physical chemistry, neurological degenerative disorders, and human evolutionary studies dealing with isolated populations. Additional interests lie in child behavior, development, and nervous system patterning and learning in primitive cultures. P.P.S.

Galactic In medicine, galactic refers to that which helps or increases the flow of MILK. In astronomy, galactic refers to a galaxy.

Galapagos Islands These 18 islands in the Pacific Ocean are on the equator. They are about 600 miles (965.61 kilometers) off the coast of South America.

The islands were formed 2 or 3 million years ago from VOLCANOES. The black lava looked like a slag heap. All living things were brought there by wind or water. This led to a strange assortment of plants and animals. The aquatic birds arrived first, making nests on the rocky ground and getting food from the ocean. Life varies on each island. Plants include brushwood, low trees, bracken ferns, prickley pear, and pampas. Animals include a variety of birds; some reptiles, especially the tortoise; seals, mantas, and sea lions, but no amphibians.

Charles Darwin came to these islands in 1835. He used his plant and animal observations as a basis for his theory of EVOLUTION, especially where it concerns the geographical distribution of species. In 1839 he wrote his famous *Origin of the Species.* H.J.C.

Galaxy A galaxy is a huge mass or system of STARS, interstellar dust, and gas. The system rotates about its axis and individual stars also move within the system.

SEE: MILKY WAY, SOLAR SYSTEM, UNIVERSE

Galaxies are systems of stars, many of which have two spiral star-arms

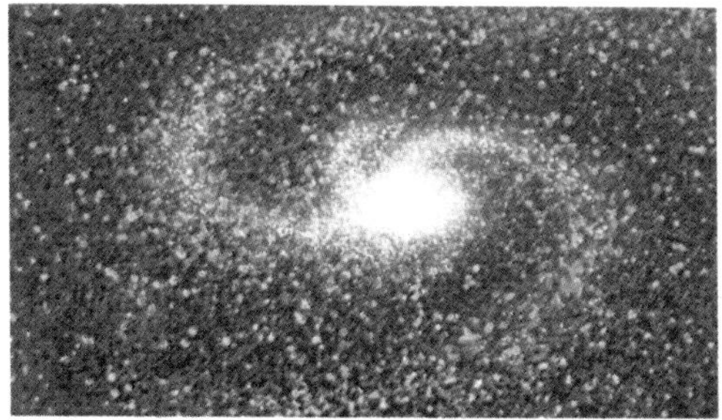

Gale A gale is a wind that blows faster than a strong breeze. There are four stages or kinds of gales, depending upon the wind speed. They range from a moderate gale to a full or whole gale.

On the BEAUFORT SCALE, winds with values of 7 to 10 on the scale are classified as gale winds.

Number 7 indicates a moderate gale and has wind velocities of 32-38 miles (51.5-61.6 kilometers) per hour. A fresh gale (number 8) has wind speeds of 39-46 miles (62.8-74.0 kilometers) per hour, while a strong gale (number 9) has speeds of 47-54 miles (75.6-86.9 kilometers) per hour. The strongest of all the gales is the full gale (number 10) with speeds of 55-63 miles (88.5-101.4 kilometers) per hour. H.S.G.

SEE ALSO: WEATHER, WEATHER FORECASTING, WIND VANE

Galen (GAY-len) (131-200 A.D.) Galen was a famous Greek physician. He lived in a time when it was illegal to dissect the human body, but he learned by dissecting lower mammals. He learned that blood is carried through the arteries and pumped by the heart, though he did not know just how it was circulated. It was not until centuries later that HARVEY learned how the circulatory system worked. Galen was ahead of his time in basing his theories on experience.

Like HIPPOCRATES, Galen believed that the human body was made up of four "humors": blood, phlegm, yellow bile, and black bile. He also believed that there were four elements in nature: air, fire, earth, and water. He further believed that there were four qualities in nature: heat, cold, moisture, and dryness. Thus he based his treatment of diseases on these theories. For example, if he were treating a patient for inflammation, an ailment which evidenced heat and dryness, Galen would apply coolness and moisture. Today a physician might apply wet dressings. In accordance with the same principles, he prescribed massage, exercise, and simple vegetable drugs, which today are still known as "galenicals."

It is interesting to note that Galen's fame throughout the centuries is not based on his skill and success, but rather on his research in ANATOMY and PHYSIOLOGY which laid the foundation for modern MEDICINE. Of the more than five hundred books Galen wrote, approximately eighty remain, and these have been copied and translated again and again.

SEE ALSO: HARVEY, HIPPOCRATES D. H. J.

Galena specimen

Galena (guh-LEE-nuh) Galena is a heavy, silvery-gray MINERAL. It is the most important source of LEAD. It is fairly brittle. A slight blow with a hammer will shatter galena into perfect cubes. This is one way to identify this mineral.

Galena is a compound of lead and sulfur (PbS). It is found in carbonate and limestone ROCKS, though some occurs in igneous and metamorphic rock. Galena is found in every state but mainly in the midwestern and northwestern areas. It occurs with other metals such as zinc, copper, and silver. It is 2.5 on the HARDNESS SCALE, has a specific gravity of 7.5, and a streak test shows lead gray. The cleavage is cubic where the axes of equal length break at right angles. Galena crystals were used in the old-fashioned radio sets. H. J. C.

SEE ALSO: CRYSTAL RADIO SET

Galileo Galilei

Galileo (gal-uh-LEE-oh) (1564-1642) Galileo was an Italian astronomer and physicist who has been called "the father of modern experimental science." He was born in Pisa on February 18, 1564, the same day that Michaelangelo died in Rome.

As a child Galileo Galilei showed such unusual skill in so many areas that his father could not decide how he should be educated. Finally it was decided that Galileo should become a physician. At seventeen he enrolled in the University of Pisa.

At college Galileo became known as "the wrangler" because he dared to question the teaching of ARISTOTLE. Although Galileo was extremely interested in mathematics, his father did not wish him to study it because he believed it to be a waste of time. So Galileo began to study mathematics privately until his father forbade him to do so. One day when he was nineteen and at prayer in Pisa Cathedral, Galileo became aware of a bronze lamp swinging from an arch overhead. The oscillations were at first great, but as they grew less and less, Galileo observed that they all took place in the same length of time. Using his pulse as a clock, he measured the time of each period. It occurred to him that an instrument could be constructed that would designate the rate of the pulse beat. He soon invented the *pulselogia*, which physicans quickly put to use. However, the PENDULUM was not applied to clocks for another fifty years.

After four years at Pisa, Galileo was forced to leave without receiving his doctor's degree because he was unable to pay for it and was denied a grant.

Back home, Galileo studied the works of ARCHIMEDES and wrote his first essay on hydrostatic balance. He began to be widely known for his geometrical and mechanical hypotheses. He also began to study the position of the center of gravity of solid bodies.

While a professor at Pisa, Galileo began to disprove Aristotle's law of FALLING BODIES. Legend has it that Galileo dropped balls from the tower of Pisa to disprove this law. Actually, he worked with inclined planes.

Feeling against Galileo became so intense that he was forced to resign, but he was immediately invited to accept a teaching post at the University of Padua. There he explored the Copernican theory that the sun, not Earth, was the center of the universe. His lectures were so popular that on occasion more than one thousand people crowded into his classroom to hear him.

Galileo longed for freedom from teaching so that he could devote more time to his study and research. He was making exciting discoveries in ASTRONOMY. He found that the surface of the moon was mountainous; that the Milky Way was composed of an immense number of small stars and nebulous matter; that ORION had over five hundred stars instead of seven; and that the Pleiades were thirty-six stars instead of seven. He outlined enormous volumes he wanted to write.

However, the church began to be uneasy about the excitement Galileo was creating, so the Pope called him to Rome for questioning. Four times Galileo was to be called before the Holy Inquisition. Finally after much personal anguish Galileo denied the truth of his discoveries. He was imprisoned in his own villa and denied any visitors. Every movement was watched intently.

Five years before he died, Galileo became blind. No longer could he study the heavens and speculate with mathematical formulae. A broken, miserable, unhappy man, Galileo waited for death. When it finally did come, his body was quickly buried in an obscure corner of a side chapel of Santa Croce. It was not until a century later that his bones were moved to a more imposing spot and a beautiful monument erected over him. But more important, his works were no longer prohibited. Galileo could be recognized as the great man he was. D. H. J.

SEE ALSO: ACCELERATION, COPERNICUS

Gall A gall is an unnatural growth of plant cells around some parasite. When a *gallfly* lays its eggs on a leaf of an oak tree, the plant cells soon surround this irritation. When the insect hatches out, the tiny larval grub uses the gall for food.

Galls take various shapes and sizes. They develop in response to a growth hormone secreted by the parasite. Other plants, such as fungi and bacteria, and animals, such as midges, aphids, flys and wasps, cause galls.

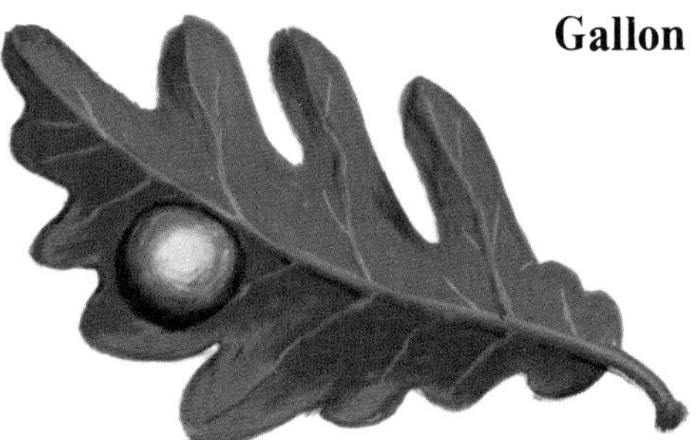

Gall on an oak leaf

Man has found a use for the *gall-nuts* on an oak which are caused by an insect (*Cynips*). They contain sufficient tannic acid to permit extraction. It is used in inks and medicines. H. J. C.

Gallbladder This is a pear-shaped sac located on the undersurface of the LIVER. It stores bile secreted by the liver. When the sac contracts, bile enters the small intestine.

Bile flows through the *cystic duct* which joins the *hepatic duct* from the liver. They form the *common bile duct* emptying into the intestine. Emptying of the gallbladder is controlled by nerves from the AUTONOMIC NERVOUS SYSTEM and by a hormone secreted by the small intestine.

The sac is lined with columnar cells resting on CONNECTIVE TISSUE, SMOOTH MUSCLE, and a covering of more connective tissue.

SEE ALSO: DIGESTIVE SYSTEM J. C. K.

Gallium (GAL-ee-um) Gallium is ELEMENT number 31. It was discovered in 1875 by Paul Lecoq de Boisbaudran. The name *gallium* comes from *Gaul* or *Galli,* part of the Roman Empire which is now France.

Gallium is a rather peculiar METAL. It has such a low MELTING POINT that if it were held in the palm of a hand, it would turn to liquid. It has an atomic weight of 69.72 and its symbol is Ga.

DIMITRI MENDELEEV, in building up the periodic table, predicted the existence and properties of elements where blank spaces existed in the table. One of these blanks was assigned the theoretical name *eka-aluminum* since it lay in the space beyond ALUMINUM. After its discovery the element was named gallium. J. R. S.

Gallon see Measurement

Gallstones When a person is eating, a liquid called *bile* flows from the liver into the digestive tract. Between meals, bile is stored in a sac called the *gall bladder*. Just as flour forms lumps in water, parts of the bile sometimes separate out to form lumps which increase in size. If the lumps (gallstones) are pushed out of the gall bladder, they stop the bile from flowing.

All gallstones possess a central core of bacteria or bile ingredients (cholesterol or calcium salts). PRECIPITATION continues around this core. A new drug, taken by mouth, can dissolve certain gallstones. However, the gallbladder and the stones are usually surgically removed to avoid infection or JAUNDICE. E.P.L./E.S.S.

SEE ALSO: DIGESTIVE SYSTEM

Galton, Sir Francis (1822-1911) Francis Galton was an English explorer and scientist who is best known as the founder of *eugenics*. This is the science that deals with the influences that improve the quality of HEREDITY of the human species by selective parenthood. He also made many contributions to the sciences of meteorology and anthropology.

Of Quaker ancestry, Galton was a cousin of CHARLES DARWIN. He was educated at King's College in London, Trinity College in Cambridge, and St. George's Hospital in London.

After making a long exploratory tour through Africa, Galton settled in London, and devoted himself to the science of eugenics. In his great book *Hereditary Genius,* he analyzed men of famous families. He later did a monumental piece of work on identical twins and sterility in marriage.

In 1863 Galton coined the term *anticyclones* as he was studying METEOROLOGY. He published articles on cyclones and weather charts which are the basis of modern weather maps. Galton also was a pioneer in the use of fingerprints for personal identification.

Galton was knighted two years before he died in 1911. D. H. J.

Luigi Galvani started electrophysiology

Galvani, Luigi (gahl-VAHN-ee, loo-EE-gee) (1737-1798) Galvani was an Italian physician and physiologist. He is most famous for his study of electricity and its relation to the physiology of living organisms.

Dr. Galvani was always interested in electricity and hoped to find a way to cure nervous disorders electrically. One day at the University of Bologna, he accidentally discovered that electric current would flow through a dead frog's legs when two different metals were connected to them. When the metals were then joined to set up a circuit, the electric current would cause the frog's legs to twitch or jump. The leg movement then could be used to indicate amounts of electric current.

Galvani wondered whether his observations about the frog meant that living organisms were a source of electricity. Galvani's metallic arc actually led him very close to the theory of the electric battery, which Volta later discovered. *Galvanism, galvanometer,* and *galvanic* are some of the electrical terms that come from Galvani's name. C. L. K.

SEE ALSO: VOLTA, ALESSANDRO

Galvanic cell see Battery

Galvanometer (gal-vuh-NAHM-uh-ter) A galvanometer is an instrument which is used to measure the strength and direction of an electric current. There are two types of galvanometers: one in which the coil moves and the magnet is fixed, and the other in which the coil is fixed and the magnet moves.

✳ **THINGS TO DO**

CAN YOU MAKE AN INSTRUMENT TO DETECT AN ELECTRIC CURRENT?

1 **Cut an end out of an empty salt box and wrap about 25 feet of bell wire around it. Leave one foot of the wire ends free.** 25′ = 7.5 m.
2 **Nail two small pieces of wood on to a block of wood. The coil of wire will lie on this base.**
3 **Magnetize a thin finishing nail by stroking one end on the south end of a bar magnet. Stroke the other end of the nail on the north end of the bar magnet.**
4 **Tie a string around the nail and tape the other end of the string to the top of the salt box.**
5 **The apparatus you have just made is a galvanometer. Place the galvanometer parallel to the earth's poles.**
6 **Connect the two ends of wire from the coil to a dry cell. The nail will swing to a position parallel to the coil of wire.**

The *fixed coil,* or Kelvin, galvanometer is the more sensitive of the two. A group of very short magnetic needles is fixed on a wire at South-North inside a coil of wire. A similar group of magnets, with reversed (N-S) polarity, is nearby. The coil is wound in reverse so that the twisting force on the MAGNETS will be in the same direction when the current flows. A bar magnet below the suspension puts a directive TORQUE on the needles so that the galvanometer has a definite zero position when no current is flowing through the coils. The deviation from zero is measured by a beam of light reflected from a mirror fixed on a suspension wire. This instrument has the serious disadvantage of being affected by stray magnetic fields.

The *moving coil* galvanometer works just the reverse of the type above. Instead of a moving magnetic suspension, it has a fixed heavy magnet with a light coil suspended in the magnetic field. This is often called a *D'Arsonval* galvanometer. A high sensitivity with this instrument calls for a coil of many turns, a concentrated magnetic field, and a delicate suspension. A. E. L.

SEE ALSO: AMMETER, ELECTRICITY, ELECTROMAGNET

Game preserve see Preserves

Gamete (GAMM-meet) A gamete is a sex cell, or reproductive cell. It can unite with another gamete to make a new cell from which an individual develops. In mammals, the union of the SPERM, or male gamete, with an OVUM, or female gamete, is the conception, or beginning, of a new animal.

SEE: EMBRYOLOGY; REPRODUCTION, SEXUAL; REPRODUCTIVE SYSTEMS; SEX

Gametophyte (gah-MEE-toh-fyte) A plant that produces gametes, the male and female sex cells, is called a *gametophyte.* Some plants will reproduce one new generation without male and female cells and then require two gametes or both male and female cells for the next generation.

The gametophyte generation of the plants usually does not look at all like the other generation, and it may be hard to realize that one plant produced the other. FERNS, MOSSES, and most of the higher plants have a gametophyte generation. J. D. B.

SEE ALSO: ALTERNATION OF GENERATIONS, PLANT, SPOROPHYTE

Gamma globulin Gamma globulin is the PROTEIN component of the human blood serum which contains the most antibodies. It is therefore effective in giving IMMUNITY to certain diseases such as mumps and measles.
SEE: ANTIBODY, BLOOD

Gamma ray see Nuclear science glossary; Ray, gamma

Gander see Fowl, Goose

Ganglion A ganglion (plural: ganglia) is a group of cell bodies of NERVE CELLS surrounded by a connective tissue capsule. It is outside the NERVOUS SYSTEM. Cell bodies inside lack capsules.

Gangrene Gangrene is a serious disease. It may result from a blood clot in an ARTERY or from an infection. If a blood clot stops the flow of blood to a part of the body, no more oxygen can nourish the tissues. The affected part dies and turns black.

Gangrene of the foot is a complication of DIABETES and ARTERIOSCLEROSIS, or it may be the result of an infection. The foot might have to be amputated. *Gas gangrene* is caused by infection of a wound with aerobic BACTERIA that exist in the soil. They need free oxygen. These organisms produce bubbles of gas throughout the tissues and may cause the death of a person. B. M. H.

Gannet The gannet is a large sea BIRD found on the rocky coasts of the Atlantic. They are white with black wing feathers. Some types are called *boobies.* They are quite tame.

Gar This is a long, slender, freshwater fish living in eastern North and Central America. It has diamond-shaped scales that do not overlap.

Gars have several primitive features. The backbone extends into the tail fin. The inner intestinal surface is increased by a spiral valve. Hard ganoid scales form an armor and the vertebrae join by ball and socket JOINTS. If oxygen in the water is low, they can breathe with their swim bladders.

They all have long jaws although one group, with shorter jaws, is named the shortnose gar. They belong to the family Lepisosteidae. J. C. K.

Garbage Any object or material not wanted any more ends up as garbage. Americans throw away 75 million tons of wastes every year. This averages to almost 2,000 pounds (907.18 kilograms) per person.

Garbage dumps are full of cast-off objects—cans, bottles, junk, old cars. Most solid wastes are dumped into open pits. This pollutes water and land.

There are no easy solutions to "the garbage problem." It requires increased technical and scientific study. Properly designed and controlled sanitary landfills are necessary. Installing ELECTROSTATIC PRECIPITATORS on all incinerator smokestacks would cut down on air pollution when combustible materials are burned. Organic wastes should be composted to permit the decomposers to reduce this garbage. (Experimental plants have already been established.) All glass and metal containers should be recycled. Refuse should be used for land reclamation. Consumers must be required to separate garbage to facilitate collection for recycling. H.J.C.

Gardenia The gardenia is a very sweet-smelling, white or pale yellow flower that grows on a bush. Gardenia petals are smooth and waxy looking.

The gardenia bush was brought from the tropics and now is cultivated chiefly in greenhouses where the air is warm and damp. The bush also grows well in gardens in southern states, along the Gulf of Mexico, and along the southern parts of the east and west coast. No other plant grown in the garden has so much fragrance.

Varieties of the gardenia bush grow from 4 to 8 feet (1.22 to 2.44 meters) high. The Gardenia jasmine is a favorite.

Gardenia plants require acid, iron-rich soil, high humidity, and plenty of sunlight and water. Propagation is done by taking cuttings from the mature plant. H.J.C.
SEE ALSO: PLANTS, TROPICAL

Photos by Helen J. Challand

Informal but planned home flower gardens

Gardening A garden is a plot of ground used for raising such plants as flowers, vegetables, or herbs. Plants in gardens can be grown and cared for in an orderly way. Gardeners help nature. They try to provide the best possible growing conditions for plants. Gardeners often collect and experiment with plants and seeds. They attempt to improve and change old varieties of plants. Each year many new varieties are introduced.

Gardening was important in the progress of mankind. Early man roamed from place to place searching for plant food to eat, until he discovered how to garden. Then he was able to stay in one place and grow his food, and build a safe home. This protection and nearby food supply gave him time to experiment with raising plants. In this way he improved his supply and variety of goods. Later, gardens were grown for beauty as well as for food. In ancient times the Hanging Gardens of Babylon were constructed. They later became known as one of the Seven Wonders of the World. King Nebuchadnezzar had these famous gardens built for his queen who missed the hilly country of her homeland. The gardens were built in the shape of a pyramid and were planted with shrubs, trees, and flowers.

INDOOR GARDENS

For centuries man has experimented with taking flora from the outside and bringing it indoors—into homes, classrooms and greenhouses. Three problems occur in this artificial setting. It is usually too warm, too dry, and too dark. However, these handicaps can be overcome by careful selection of house plants and scientific care. Plants should be placed in southern light. Since window glass cuts out part of the sun's rays, artificial light may be provided when days become shorter. Homemade greenhouses, of course, furnish a greater area for light to enter.

Ferns, cyclamen, African violets, and other plants should not be in direct light. Other plants, if deprived of sufficient light, will grow long spindly stems, drop leaves, and fail to bloom. The temperature should be in the upper 60's and lower 70's (from 19° C. to 22° C.) during the day and in the upper 50's (about 14° C.) at night. Plants need water. However, over-watering will fill the air spaces in the soil and prevent roots from getting oxygen. When dusty, leaves should be washed.

ROCK GARDENS

A rock garden is like a little bit of mountainside brought down into the valley. Weathered limestone or other porous rock will make a good setting for rock-garden plants. A volcanic rock called *tuffa* is full of holes in which roots can attach. Good drainage can be arranged by beginning with a layer of gravel, then sand and topping with a generous amount of rich loam. Plants selected from the alpine group are miniature, shrubby and colorful. The flowers bloom profusely and over a short period of time. Since they grow up on mountains and rocky slopes, they have a shorter growing period. During the winter, the garden should be covered with a thick layer of leaves or hay to prevent alternate freezing and thawing.

PLANNING FOR FLOWERS

A good garden plan on paper shows where different plants will be located and how far apart. Gardeners may select annuals, perennials, biennials, bulbs and woody plants. ANNUALS like marigolds, zinnias, and petunias grow rapidly from seed but live for only one growing season. Hollyhocks, and sweet William are BIENNIALS and live for two years, usually blooming or bearing seeds the second year. PERENNIALS are plants that live for many years. Tender perennials like GERANIUMS and marguerites can be killed by frost. Hardy perennials such as IRIS and peonies resist severe cold. BULBS, tubers, corms, and rhizomes are usually perennials. Tulips, gladiolus, begonias, and dahlias are among this group. Woody plants include shrubs, trees, and some VINES. These hard-stemmed plants live for many years.

The gardener should select some plants that will flower in spring, others that are summer blooming, and still others that bloom in the fall. Pleasing color combinations should be planned and mature size and height of plants are important to the appearance of the garden. Tall flowers should be placed well back in the garden or border, with medium varieties in the middle, and small plants in front. Tall plants in windy places should be staked to prevent breaking. Flowers are usually planted in clumps rather than rows for a more attractive display. Crocus, snowdrops, daffodils, bachelor buttons, marigolds, nasturtiums, petunias, zinnias, violas, and forget-me-nots are easily raised by the beginning gardener.

VEGETABLE GARDENS

Herb, kitchen, market, and truck gardens supply man with food. Vegetables raised in market gardens are sold to nearby stores and markets.

Large VEGETABLE gardens are truck gardens from which produce is shipped to distant wholesale markets. Vegetables raised in kitchen or home gardens are for family use. The type of garden depends on the kinds of vegetables that thrive in the area, the location of the garden, its size, type of soil, and the climate.

Herbs, raised for market or home use, are used as food flavoring, in medicines, candy, perfumes, or as tea. Basil, sage, thyme, lavender, and mint are a few herbs that can be raised in home herb gardens.

Kitchen gardens provide delicious, select, low cost vegetables. Some vegetables, such as corn, peas, and lettuce lose much of their fresh flavor soon after they are harvested. Vegetables raised in the home garden can be eaten right after they reach maturity and are picked. Tomatoes that are vine-ripened have a more delicious flavor than those sent to markets. Unusual, delicate, or rare varieties of vegetables can be raised by the home gardener.

Design of a vegetable and herb garden. (1 foot equals .3 meter and 1 inch equals 2.54 centimeters.)

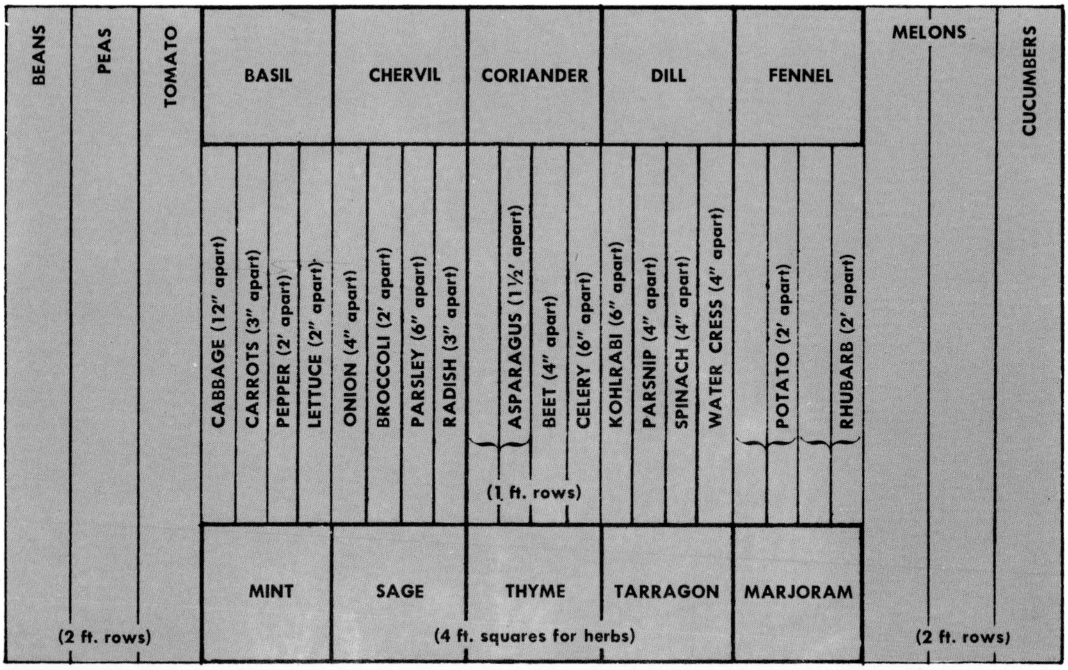

BEANS
PEAS
TOMATO
BASIL
CHERVIL
CORIANDER
DILL
FENNEL
MELONS
CUCUMBERS
CABBAGE (12" apart)
CARROTS (3" apart)
PEPPER (2' apart)
LETTUCE (2" apart)
ONION (4" apart)
BROCCOLI (2' apart)
PARSLEY (6" apart)
RADISH (3" apart)
ASPARAGUS (1½' apart)
BEET (4" apart)
CELERY (6" apart)
KOHLRABI (6" apart)
PARSNIP (4" apart)
SPINACH (4" apart)
WATER CRESS (4" apart)
POTATO (2' apart)
RHUBARB (2' apart)
(1 ft. rows)
MINT
SAGE
THYME
TARRAGON
MARJORAM
(2 ft. rows)
(4 ft. squares for herbs)
(2 ft. rows)

PLANNING VEGETABLE GARDENS

A good vegetable garden should be planned on paper to show the crops that will be raised, the space they will occupy, and the distance between rows. Rows should run across sloping ground to help prevent soil EROSION. Crops that grow at the same speed and height should be planted near each other. After they are harvested new crops can be planted in their place. This is called *successive planting*. Leaf lettuce, radishes, beets, carrots, beans, onion sets, and tomato plants are good selections for the beginning vegetable gardener. The soil must be spaded from 6 to 8 inches (15.24 to 20.32 centimeters) deep and large clods of earth broken into small pieces. HUMUS should be added so the soil will be soft and workable. FERTILIZER adds chemicals that will supply food for the growing plants. Stable manure acts as humus and fertilizer. The surface layer of soil should be raked smooth before seeds or plants are set out.

Information on hardy plants for specific regions, planting times, diseases and pest control, and how to improve soil, can be obtained from the state agricultural experimental stations, nurseries, state colleges, local garden centers, seed catalogs, and seed or plant packages. Seed sown directly in the garden is scattered in a drill or shallow trench. More seeds are sown than are needed because not every seed will grow. Seedlings should be thinned out and transplanted when the first true leaves appear. Seedbeds must be kept moist. Rows should be clearly marked with stakes.

Plants can be started indoors in flats. Seeds should be planted in moist, sterile soil in flats, and covered with glass. Newspaper placed over the glass keeps the light out. As the seedlings develop, the newspaper and glass are removed. About a week before the plants are to be set out, they should be hardened by placing the flats out-of-doors during the daytime.

The garden should be cultivated about once a week to keep the soil soft and kill weeds. The garden should be watered whenever necessary. Plants should be sprayed to protect them from insect pests and diseases.

M. R. L.

SEE ALSO: AGRICULTURE, BULB, CORMS, CULTIVATION, EROSION, GREENHOUSE, PLANT, PLANT DISEASES, RHIZOME, TUBER

The garlic plant and its compound bulb

Garlic Garlic is a well-known HERB. People have used this plant to flavor food for thousands of years.

Strong-smelling garlic is a relative of both the ONION and LILY. It is a perennial plant, about 20 inches (50.8 centimeters) tall, growing from a bulb. Unlike the onion, the garlic BULB is compound. It consists of several *bulblets,* or *cloves,* all of which are enclosed in one, thin sheath. In autumn, the plant is dug up and the bulb dried. The cloves are used for seasoning, PROPAGATION, and certain medicines.

J.A.D.

Red pyrope garnet

Garnet Garnets are members of a group of minerals containing silicon and oxygen (silicate) combined with the metals calcium, magnesium, iron, and aluminum. The best-known garnets are the deep red ones used in jewelry. "Garnet" means "pomegranate," which has seeds the color of some varieties of the mineral. However, garnets also occur in other colors.

Because of their hardness, garnets are often used in making ABRASIVE papers and watch jewels. Garnets are widely distributed throughout the world and are found in both metamorphic and igneous ROCKS.

Varieties of garnet include pyrope and almandite (precious garnets) as used in jewelry, grossularite (white to brown), spessartite (sometimes violet-tinted), andradite (yellow, green, red, black), and uvarovite (green).

D.J.I.

SEE ALSO: GEM, MINERALS

Garter snake see Snakes

✳ **THINGS TO DO**

WHICH GAS IS LIGHTER THAN AIR? WHICH ONE IS HEAVIER?

Do this only with the help of an adult.

1 **Fill a balloon with carbon dioxide. To do this, pour two inches of vinegar into a pop bottle. Put two tablespoons of soda into this and immediately pull the mouth of a balloon over the mouth of the bottle. The balloon will fill up with carbon dioxide. Tie the balloon.**

2 **Fill a second balloon with hydrogen. To do this, put several strips of zinc in the bottom of a pop bottle. Pour a dilute solution of hydrochloric acid into the bottle. Avoid getting any of the acid on your hands or clothes. Pull the mouth of a balloon over the mouth of the bottle. Soon the balloon will fill up with hydrogen.**

3 **Hold the two balloons up in the air and release them. One balloon will descend and the other one will ascend. Which gas is lighter than air? Which one is heavier than air?**

Gas Physically all matter can be classified by form as either a solid, a liquid, or a gas. These are called *states* of matter. The molecular activity determines which state a group of atoms or molecules will be. Generally, the higher the temperature, the greater is the molecular motion or activity. In a gas, the molecules bounce in all directions so that only the confining walls of a vessel will restrict the molecular motion. Thus, a gas occupies the shape and volume of its containing vessel. A liquid takes the shape of the vessel but retains its own volume. A solid has both its own shape and volume.

The gas used for fuel in automotive and aircraft engines is actually a liquid, *gasoline*. It is very *volatile,* which means that it vaporizes, or turns to a gas, very easily.

Gases, like liquids and solids, occupy space and have definite weights and the property INERTIA. It is easy to see that a solid, such as a wooden block, takes up space and weighs something. So, too, with the liquid water in a glass. But what about air (which is a mixture of certain gaseous chemicals)? A simple home experiment (as shown in the picture below) will prove that air really does take up space even though it usually cannot be seen or felt. An "empty" bottle is not really empty.

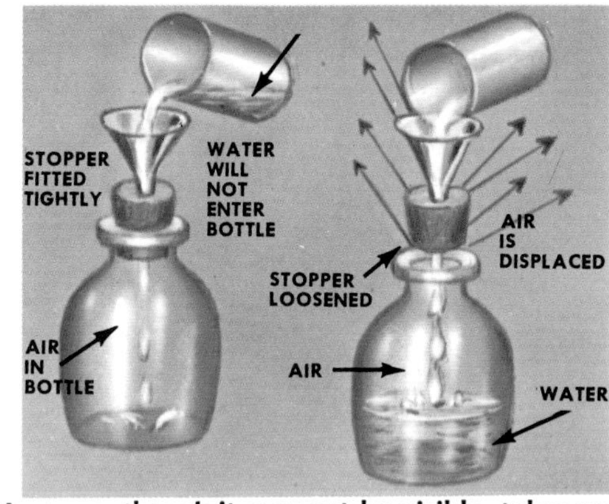

Any gas, though it may not be visible, takes up space and must be able to escape if another substance is to take its place

Compared to solids and liquids, which are relatively dense (heavy), all gases are of *low density.* A cubic foot of water weighs 62.4 pounds, (1 gram per cubic centimeter) but a cubic foot of air weighs only 1¼ ounces (1¼ grams per liter).

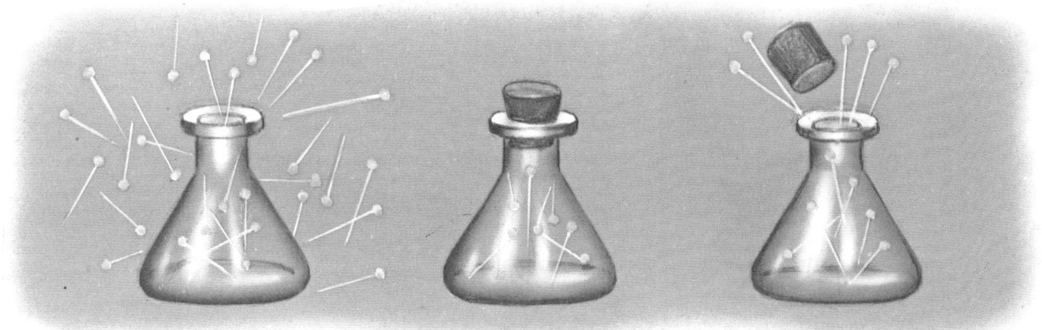

An unstoppered flask in a room of air has equal amounts of pressure inside and out. If the flask is stoppered and put in a vacuum (airless space), the air in the flask still has pressure. When the air is released into the vacuum, the air molecules bounce away

Liquids and solids are, in general, easily visible—even clear ones such as water and ice; but most gases are colorless and invisible. Air is a mixture of several colorless gases, chiefly oxygen, nitrogen, water vapor, and carbon dioxide. But chlorine is a yellow gas, and the hot vapor of iodine is deep purple. Many gases have a distinctive odor—as chlorine or cooking gas. Automobiles give off the dangerous but odorless gas, CARBON MONOXIDE.

Another characteristic of a gas is its ability to *diffuse*. One gas easily passes through another. The molecules of two or more kinds of gases mix more readily than do other forms of matter. When carbon monoxide from an auto in a closed garage mixes with air, the two gases have diffused together and it is dangerous for a person to breathe the air containing carbon monoxide.

THE KINETIC THEORY APPLIED TO GASES

Important actions of gases are explained by the KINETIC (*molecular*) THEORY. By this theory, all substances are made of many extremely small particles or MOLECULES, each particle not visible by itself. Each molecule is in constant motion; and the many such particles making up the gas within a container are constantly bouncing about like excited bees in a bottle, or like animated ping pong balls. As they move about, they often hit against one another and against the walls of the container. The warmer the gas, the harder they hit; and thus the whole effect is to produce a *pressure* of the gas against the enclosing walls. In solids and liquids, the molecules also move about, but less actively; and they are closer together than in gases. This kinetic theory helps explain and predict many kinds of gas behavior, including the gas laws, diffusion, and expansion by heat.

KINETIC THEORY AND UNDERSTANDING EXPLOSIONS

If one measures the diameter of a balloon filled with air at room temperature, and then warms the balloon, it will be seen to increase in diameter. The molecules move faster and farther apart on being heated; thus they expand the elastic walls of the balloon. If they were enclosed in a rigid vessel, the pressure would increase.

Explosions are caused by a similar but faster expansion of heated gases. For example, when gunpowder or gasoline vapor burn, it is the kinetic energy of motion of hot, high-speed gas molecules that causes this vapor to perform its explosive work.

Gas may be changed to a liquid by cooling. This process is called *change of state*. The temperature at which a liquid changes to a gas is called its *boiling point*. Water is an example of change of state from a liquid to a gas. If water is boiled in a kettle, steam comes from the spout. Steam, or water vapor, is the gas produced when water is heated above 212° F. (100° C.). If a cool pie tin is held several inches from the spout, water collects on the tin. Steam, cooled below 212° F. (100° C.), forms water.

Water is often purified by this process of boiling water and then cooling the steam. This process is called DISTILLATION. Water vapor is also a form of gas found in the air. When the air is cooled, the water vapor changes to droplets of water. Water collects on the outside of a glass of cold water on a warm day. The air around the glass is cooled, and water is released.

Very cold temperatures are required to

change some gases into liquid. For example, air must be cooled to −300° F. (−184.4° C.) in order to become liquid. Helium must be cooled to −450° F. (−267.8° C.) to become a liquid.

GAS LAWS

Several basic laws have been discovered by scientists to describe the observable behavior of gases. These laws were worked on bv Amedeo Avogadro, Robert Boyle and Jacques Charles, Joseph Gay-Lussac and Joseph Henry.

Avogadro's Law states that equal volumes of any different gases at the same temperature contain an equal number of molecules. This principle is employed in a method of determining atomic weights.

Boyle's Law states that when a gas is compressed into a smaller space, internal pressure increases. According to this law, if the temperature of a gas remains the same, the smaller the space confining the gas, the greater is the pressure exerted by the gas. Pressure is in direct proportion to the density of the gas. If the gas is pressed into one third of its original space, the amount of pressure, or push, on the walls of the container increases three times. Within this space is confined the original number of molecules, now moving within the decreased area of the container.

Charles' Law states that when a gas is heated, the molecules move more rapidly and therefore hit the sides of the container more often. This means the gas in the container is exerting more pressure. Gas, like most other matter, expands when it is heated and contracts when it is cooled. Charles stated that when a gas is kept at the same pressure and then heated, the gas expands by 1/273 of its volume at 0°C. (32°F.) for every one degree C. rise in temperature.

Henry's Law states that the weight of a given gas which will dissolve in a given amount of water is directly proportional to the pressure of the gas.

Gases differ a great deal in the degree to which they will dissolve in water. In limited amounts, hydrogen, oxygen, carbon monoxide, and nitrogen are soluble in water. OXYGEN at room temperature will dissolve at the approximate ratio of three parts of oxygen to 100 parts of water. It is such dissolved oxygen that fish and other water animals breathe in water. CARBON DIOXIDE, hydrogen sulfide, and chlorine are examples of gases which are moderately soluble in water. Plants growing in water use carbon dioxide. Sulfur dioxide, hydrogen chloride, and ammonia are examples of highly water-soluble gases. AMMONIA used in homes for cleaning purposes is dissolved in water. Hydrogen chloride is dissolved in water to obtain hydrochloric acid.

SOME USES OF GASES

Life itself would not be possible without gases. Both plant and animal life are dependent upon oxygen and carbon dioxide for survival. Natural and manufactured gases are delivered to homes for cooking, heating, and other uses. Refrigerators and air-conditioners use ammonia, gases, freon, or similar items during the cooling-heating cycle. Some gases (helium, argon, neon, krypton, and mercury vapor) are used for electric signs and fluorescent lights. Air is used for air brakes, air hammers, drills, and atomizers.

Steam turbines and automobiles use a gas for their operation. In medicine, gases are used to kill bacteria, to anesthetize, and to enrich the oxygen intake of a patient.

In chemical warfare or riot control several gases are used such as nerve gas, depressant gas, and hallucinatory gas. International peace organizations try to control their manufacture and use. P. F. D.

SEE ALSO: CHLORINE, COAL GAS, EXPANSION, GAY-LUSSAC'S GAS LAW, NATURAL GAS, PHYSICAL STATES AND CHANGES

Gasoline see Engine, Ethyl, Fuel

Gastric juice see Digestive system

Gastrovascular cavity (gas-tro-VASS-kyuh-ler) The gastrovascular cavity is the central body cavity of an animal such as a coelenterate. It functions in both digestion and circulation.

SEE ALSO: COELENTERATA, HYDRA

Gastrula see Embryology

Gauge A gauge is a device for measuring quantities, such as the steam pressure inside a boiler, the liquid level of a container, the thickness of a wire. Complex machines have many gauges. "Gauge" also means a standard measure, such as the distance between two rails of a railway.

SEE: RAIN GAUGE, SNOW GAUGE

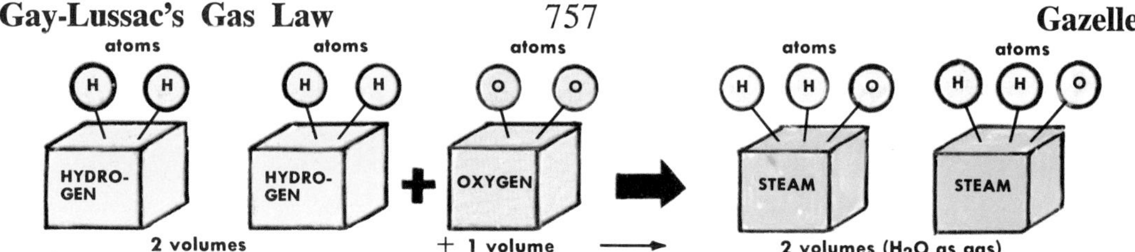

Gay-Lussac observed that gases combine in simple proportions

Gay-Lussac's Gas Law (geh-luh-SAHK) When gases combine or react together to form a new substance, they do so in simple proportions by volume. For instance, steam (the gaseous form of water) is made up of two gases, hydrogen and oxygen. If two volumes of hydrogen gas are combined with one volume of oxygen gas, exactly two volumes of steam will result. If one volume of hydrogen is combined with one volume of chlorine, two volumes of hydrogen chloride are produced. If one volume nitrogen and three volumes hydrogen combine, the result is two volumes of ammonia gas.

Gas reactions such as these were observed by Joseph Gay-Lussac, a French chemist who lived from 1778-1850. In 1808, he put these observations together to form a law which bears his name. Gay-Lussac's Law states that the relation between the combining volumes of gases and the volume of their products (if they are two gases) may be expressed in small, whole numbers. This law, also called the *Law of Combining Gases,* is one of the most important in CHEMISTRY. Restated it says: Volumes of gases in any chemical change bear a simple ratio to one another under the same conditions of temperature and pressure.

In 1811, the gas law of Gay-Lussac led an Italian, Amedeo Avogadro, to advance an explanation or hypothesis as to why gases combine in simple volume ratios. Specifically, his hypothesis explained *why* two volumes of hydrogen unite with one volume of oxygen to make two (not three) volumes of water vapor, and *why* three volumes of hydrogen and one volume nitrogen make two volumes of ammonia gas. Up until this time, no one had considered that a gas molecule might consist of two atoms. But Avogadro reasoned that if it did, Gay-Lussac's law of combining volumes could be explained. Thus graphically: Measurements of other gas combinations confirmed Avogadro's assumption that the molecules of common gases are composed of two atoms each.

This assumption, combined with Boyle's and Charles' gas laws, led Avogadro to state that all gases behave alike because equal volumes of all gases under the same conditions of temperature and pressure contain the same number of molecules. Much later the actual number of molecules in a given volume of any gas was determined.

H. W. M.

SEE ALSO: BOYLE'S LAW, CHARLES' LAW, GAS, MOLECULE

Gazelle There are many species of gazelles, all of them living in either Africa or Asia. They are slender-legged and graceful. Their short horns point backward, are ringed with ridges, and are present in both sexes.

Gazelles differ from other antelopes by their small size, large shining eyes, and great abundance. Often they live in herds consisting of a male and a number of females. When young males are eight months old, they are forced to leave the herd. They form bachelor herds of varying sizes.

Gazelles are cud chewers (*ruminants*) related to cattle, sheep, and goats. J. C. K.

SEE ALSO: ANTELOPE, DEER FAMILY

Dik-dik, a small gazelle of Africa's dry areas

Chicago Natural History Museum

Gear A gear is a mechanical device which carries or transmits ENERGY so that one moving part of a machine makes other parts move. Gears can change the direction of MOTION and increase or decrease torque, depending on their relative size and arrangement.

SEE: MACHINERY

Gecko see Lizards

Geiger counter (GYE-guhr) The Geiger-Müller counter shows the presence of radioactive rays by giving off a clicking sound. Radioactive particles ionize a gas within the counter tube.

In the very early days of detecting radioactive decay particles, fluorescent screens were placed over the substance under examination. Scanning the screen with a microscope, the observer could see tiny flashes of light when the decay particles struck the screen. This was a very cumbersome and inaccurate method.

Around 1900 Sir Ernest Rutherford, a British scientist, and Hans Geiger, a German physicist, observed that a gas-filled tube containing ELECTRODES could be made to produce a discharge when the potential applied to these electrodes was increased. They also found that the tube would discharge if a radioactive substance were placed near it. Thus, they developed the first radiation counter.

The Geiger-Müller tube counter, or Geiger counter as it is more commonly called, uses such a discharge tube to detect the decay particles and to count the actual number which occur per minute. The Geiger counter which is used today was developed in 1920 by Geiger and Müller.

The operation of this counter is as follows: an ionized (charged) particle traveling through the counter will knock an electron from a gas molecule in the tube. This electron will be accelerated by the electric field that exists because of the voltage on the electrodes. It will actually gain enough energy to ionize more gas molecules, thus forming an "avalanche" of electrons. This causes a pulse of electricity to flow through the tube.

If the electrodes of the tube are connected not only in series with a current source but also with an electronic amplifier, these electrical pulses can be made to operate a mechanical counter, thus recording the number of radioactive particles.

The advantage of the Geiger counter is its ability to shut itself off after each event. Thus it is automatically ready to count the next decay particle. This extremely short amount of time is called the "recovery time" of the tube or counter. In practical counters, this time should not be longer than .001 second. A. E. L.

SEE ALSO: NUCLEAR REACTORS, NUCLEAR SCIENCE

Gelatin Gelatin is a PROTEIN mixture made from bones, hoofs, connective tissue and skins of animals.

In the commercial process, the animal parts are first treated with either acid or lime, then washed to remove impurities. The gelatin is extracted by applying warm water. After filtering and drying, the gelatin is ground to a gray powder.

Refined gelatin is used in the preparation of foods, such as soups and canned meats, and drug items, such as pills and capsules. Less refined gelatin is used for photographic film, paper sizing and plastics. D. A. B.

SEE ALSO: PROTEIN

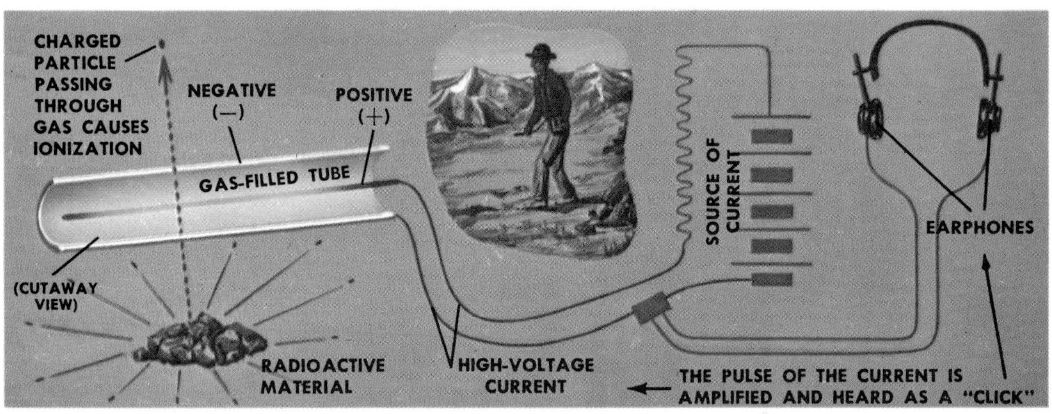

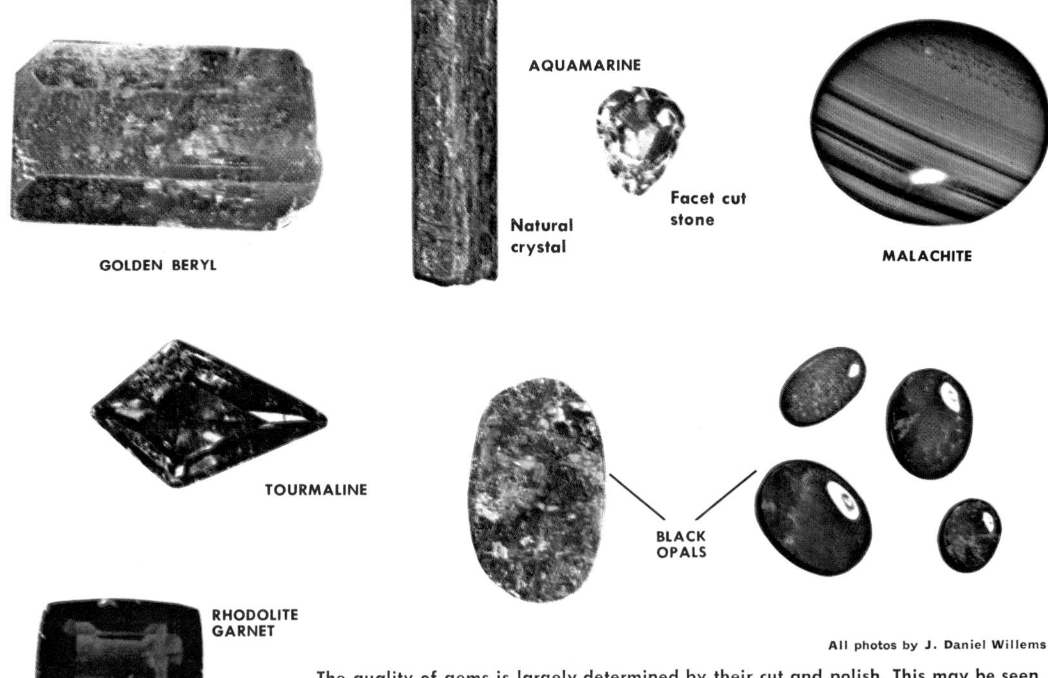

All photos by J. Daniel Willems

The quality of gems is largely determined by their cut and polish. This may be seen in the illustration by comparison of the finished aquamarine with the natural crystal from which it was cut

Gem A gem is a stone which, when cut and polished, is used in jewelry. Sometimes they are called "precious stones." Most gems are rare mineral crystals found in nature, such as diamonds, rubies, sapphires, and emeralds. Pearls and amber are classed as gems also, but they have an animal background. Gems are prized for their beauty, their hardness, which makes them last indefinitely, and their rarity. They are sold and resold from generation to generation. All ages and all races of mankind have placed great value upon them.

There are over 2,000 minerals; however, only a fraction of them are commonly used as gems. Emeralds and aquamarines are different varieties of the mineral *beryl.* Rubies and sapphires are forms of CORUNDUM (alumina). AGATE, AMETHYST, opal, and ONYX are forms of quartz. The remaining gem minerals are DIAMOND, garnet, jade, topaz, turquoise, zircon, moonstone, lapis lazuli, peridot, spinel, and TOURMALINE. From animal mineraloids, the pearl, amber, jet, and coral are classed as gems. People have been able to make substances in the laboratory with exactly the same properties as gems. These are called *synthetic gems.*

The outstanding characteristic of all gems that sets them apart from non-gem minerals is their beauty. The beauty of a gem is due to its color and brilliance. Gem minerals are usually found in nature as colorless, pure and transparent crystals. Such a mineral is the diamond. Occasionally, however, they are found with some impurities which cause them to appear colored. When the impurities are evenly distributed throughout the crystal (which occurs only rarely), a beautiful gem such as a ruby, emerald, or sapphire results.

Few gems are attractive when first taken from the earth. They must be shaped and polished by the gem cutter to bring out the beauty. The brilliance of a gem is due to the amount of light reflected. Some of the light is reflected from the surface of the crystal. Some enters the crystal, is bent or refracted, strikes an interior surface, and is reflected out the front again. The greater the amount of light reflected from the interior, the greater the brilliance. A diamond disperses more light than any other gem. A gem can be identified by the angle at which it refracts light and by its density. H.W.M.

SEE ALSO: CRYSTAL, DENSITY, MINERALS, ROCKS

Gemini, the Twins

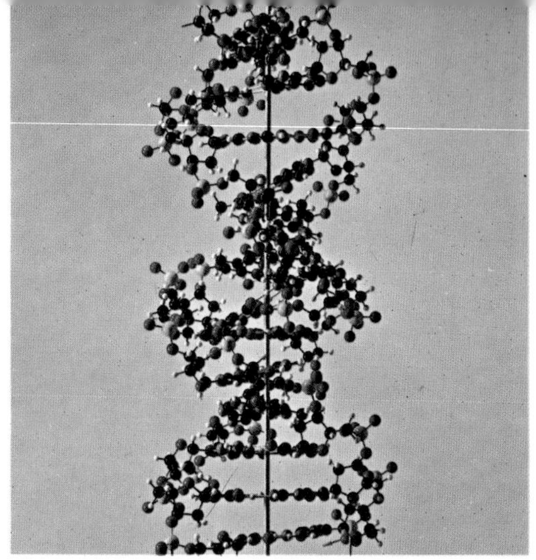

Abbott Laboratories

Arrangement of atoms in a model of DNA (deoxyribonucleic acid). A widely-held hypothesis is that DNA is the basic unit of genes

Gemini (JEM-uh-nee) Gemini means "the Twins." This CONSTELLATION is one of the signs of the ZODIAC. In winter and early spring there are two rows of stars next to each other in the sky. There is a bright star at the top of each row. Since early times these rows of stars have been imagined to represent twins.

According to the Greeks and Romans, the twins were supposed to be Castor and Pollux, twin sons of Jupiter and Leda, the wife of a king of Sparta. Castor and Pollux were sportsmen. Castor was famous for his interest in horsemanship, and Pollux was a patron of boxing. Castor was a mortal and Pollux was supposed to be immortal. When Castor died, Pollux was so grieved that Jupiter put them both in the sky together as a constellation.

Gene (JEEN) A gene is a chemical unit which alone, or working with other genes, brings about the development of one or several characteristics such as eye or skin color. Genes are parts of CHROMOSOMES.

Pairs of genes are located on pairs of chromosomes. If the pair of genes do not affect a hereditary trait in the same way, the gene which is more powerful or *dominant* determines the characteristic shown by the organism.

It is now believed that each gene controls the formation of only one protein, usually an enzyme. Genes are parts of DNA molecules.

All of the parts of an organism such as cell membranes, pigments, and tissues are composed of proteins. The making of proteins, during the processes of repair and development, involves a series of chemical reactions. Since all reactions in the body are controlled by enzymes, genes can control which reactions take place. For example, the eye of a fruit fly may be white because genes controlling enzymes necessary to the reactions involved in making a red eye are missing. Thus, the eye lacks color. J. C. K.

SEE ALSO: CELL, ENZYME, HEREDITY, PROTEIN

Generator A generator is a machine for using some natural kind of energy and changing it to electrical energy or current.

The earliest invented kind of generator, developed by MICHAEL FARADAY, was the DYNAMO. This type is still used to make the direct currents needed to charge auto batteries. A dynamo consists of several steel U-magnets that form the outer part of field. Inside, between the magnet's poles is a coil of many turns of insulated wire mounted on a rotatable bearing. This turning coil is the *armature*. In addition, a collector or commutator device is used to take off to two lead-out wires the electrical energy that is generated when some energy source actually spins the armature between the magnetic field poles.

Commonwealth Edison Co.

Dangerous radioactive wastes are stored in tanks

Commonwealth Edison Co.

High-voltage transformers at the Dresden plant prepare the power for transmission

Commonwealth Edison Co.

Control room of the Dresden, Illinois, Nuclear-energy Electric Generator Station. The nest of circular lights (upper left) record the activity of the radioactive uranium bundles. Man's hand (at center) points to "SCRAM" button which can shut down the entire generator plant in 2½ seconds, in case radioactive fission goes too fast and the plant overheats

Modern home and industrial needs for large amounts of electrical energy have led to generators differing in certain details, from the design of the simple dynamo. These modern generators deliver alternating current (A.C.) which can easily be run through TRANSFORMERS, and so altered in voltage for long-distance transmission and other special uses. These A.C. generators use—instead of permanent iron magnets—great coils of wire for their magnetic fields, as well as using coils for their armatures.

Large generators take—as their source of energy—either falling water or boiler-made steam. The most widely used electric generator stations produce their turbine-driving steam by tapping the chemical energy of burning coal.

In recent years, the latest designs of experimental generators use uranium-fueled NUCLEAR ENERGY to produce heat energy. Then, as described before, this heat boils water to change it to steam; and the steam turns turbines that, finally, spin the generator armatures and produce current. D. A. B.

SEE ALSO: ARMATURE, ELECTRICITY, MAGNET, NUCLEAR REACTOR

Genetics see Fruit fly; Heredity; Mendel, Gregor Johann

Genetic Engineering see Hybridization

Genus see Animals, classification of; Plants, classification of

Geography Geography is the science that deals with the description and location of the Earth's living organisms as well as the plotting of landforms on the Earth's surface. The term "geography" comes to us from the Greek term *geographia* which means to describe the Earth's surface. The science of geography includes the exact description of the land areas, the oceans, the characteristics of the atmosphere, and the distribution of plant and animal life, including man. Geography includes part of the natural and Earth sciences as well as social science.

The study of geography must include the influence of his surroundings on man. As man adjusts to his environment, he alters the natural pattern. He changes it with man-made schemes. This is called the *cultural environment*. Included in the cultural environment are such features on the earth's surface as cities, roads, railroads, canals, fields, dams, drainage ditches, and irrigation networks.

In the natural or *physical environment,* eight main factors should be considered: space relationships, including location; relief or topographic factors; climatic factors; soil; the flora and fauna; ground water and natural drainage conditions; the mineral resources; and the relationship with the sea.

NATURAL ENVIRONMENT

An important aspect of geography is the study of *space relationships* of different areas of the world. This involves a careful investigation of all factors that make up the environment of a location and the advantages and disadvantages of that environment. This would include such things as the natural vegetation, topography, mineral resources, and CLIMATE.

A system for determining location on the Earth has been devised. This is called the *geographic grid.* It is composed of east-west lines of LATITUDE (parallels) that extend from the equator to the poles and of north-south lines of LONGITUDE (meridians) that extend from the prime meridian which runs through Greenwich, England, to the 180th meridian. This is the International Date Line. These two different lines are called *coordinates* and are used in NAVIGATION.

The *relief* and *topography* of a region include land elevations, the amount of level land, the steepness of the slope, the type of terrain features (such as mountains, valleys, plains, and plateaus). To a great degree, the relief and topography determine how habitable the land will be and for what use the region is best suited.

The climate of a region is of great importance. It influences the types of plant and animal life, the nature of the soil, and man's use of the region. There are many factors that control climate. Among these are latitude, mountain barriers, prevailing winds, and landmass as compared to ocean areas.

The type of soil also influences the use that may be made of a region.

Flora and fauna (plants and animals) are also influenced by topography, elevation, type of bedrock, drainage and soil. In turn, the flora and fauna help to determine the soil types.

The habitability of a region is influenced by the nearness of the *ground water* to the surface. Rivers are sources or potential sources of drinking water, irrigation, sewage disposal and power. In addition to being of scenic interest, they may be routes of trade or culture, and they may serve as boundary lines.

The availability and location of mineral resources is of particular importance to a region—culturally and economically. The location of the deposits in relation to other metals and to population and transportation centers is also of great interest.

The most important effect of the OCEAN is on the climate of the world. The relationship of the area to the sea influences rainfall and temperature. Oceans are a trade and culture medium and are natural boundary zones. They also were great barriers—separating and isolating countries and continents. The sea is a rich source of supply for food. The control of the sea greatly affected political and strategic powers.

The environment of man is forever changing, both physically and culturally. The earth's surface is forever being altered by the natural process of EROSION, volcanic eruptions, landslides, EARTHQUAKES, glaciers, hurricanes, tidal waves, droughts and floods. The cultural landscape is constantly being altered by changes in the number, location, and size of towns, new roads, railroads, dams, drainage and irrigation systems, by land clearing, and by accidentally caused fires.

The field of geography may be divided in many ways. A common grouping is between the physical earth—called *physical geography,* and the study of living things, their activities, and how they affect the physical earth—called *biogeography.*

PHYSICAL GEOGRAPHY

Physical geography is the study of all physical features of the Earth. This includes the study of landforms, the atmosphere, the oceans, and the changes that are constantly taking place. Physical geography investigates the mechanical forces (*volcanism* and *diastrophism*) and the forces of weathering and erosion (*gradation*). There are many subdivisions of physical geography.

Mathematical geography deals with the numerical calculations of the earth as a PLANET in space, time, shape, and motion. It also is concerned with the accurate locations of given spots by means of a coordinate system, described in imaginary lines of parallels and meridians.

Geography

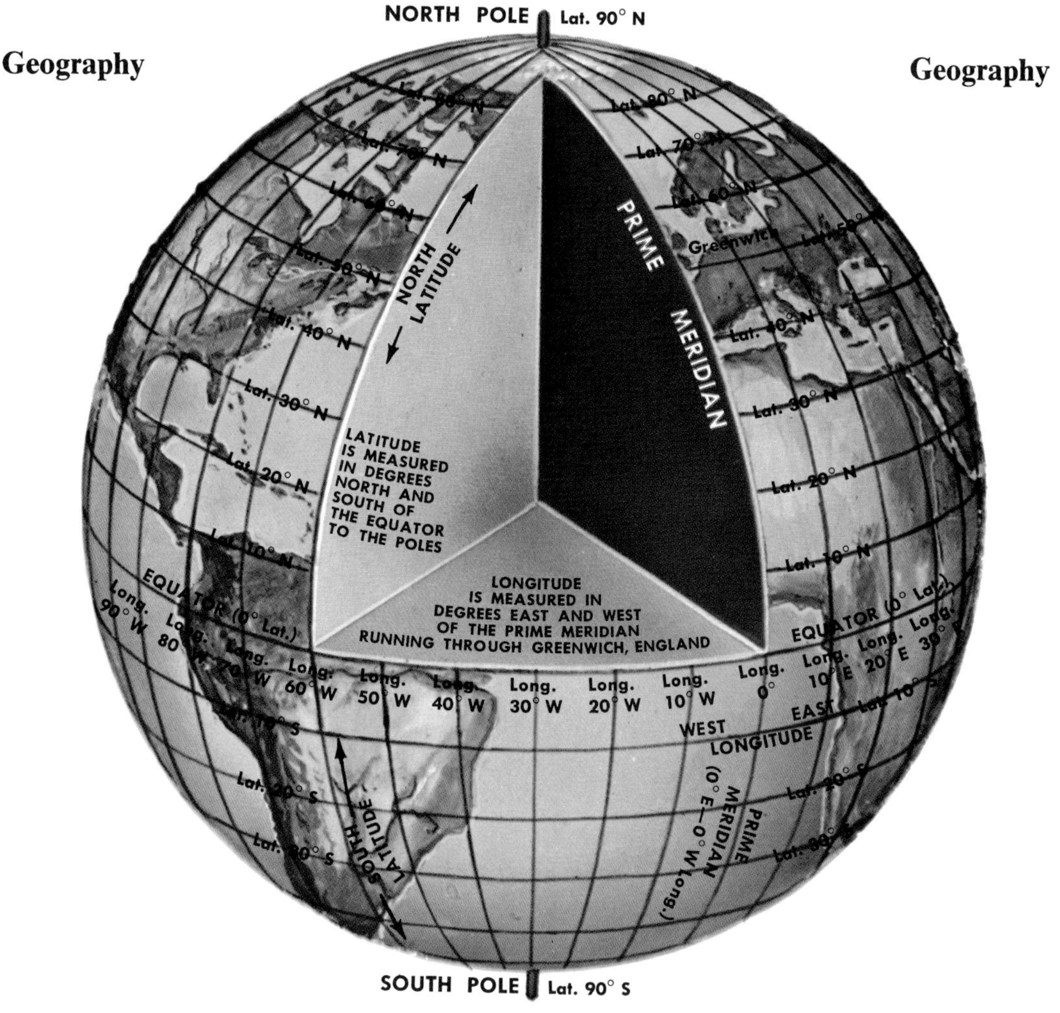

Geographers use the system of coordinates shown on the globe above to locate any place on the earth's surface. North-south measurements are from the equator to the poles, and east-west measurements are from the prime meridian to the 180th meridian.

OCEANOGRAPHY has been advanced with data collected since the International Geophysical Year. *Climatology* and *meteorology* are included in geography. Meteorology refers to all types of weather data, and climatology refers to climates.

BIOGEOGRAPHY

Biogeography is a study of relationships between living things and the surface of the earth. It is a part of, but not the whole of, the subject of plant and animal ECOLOGY. The ecologist also studies biotic communities, populations, and environments which function or work together as ecosystems.

The geography of an environment as a factor that influences an ECOSYSTEM is important to an ecologist. For instance, geographic isolation produced in a valley surrounded by high mountain barriers has a profound effect upon plants and animals in the ecosystem. Population density, animal competition, genetic factors of inbreeding and survival of mutations are all affected by geography of the region.

Sometimes population density and migration may be primarily controlled by physical geographical factors such as temperature, rainfall and availability of streams and waterholes. At other times, major controlling factors may be biological ones such as succession, predator-prey relationships and competition.

Man is an animal able to control or adapt to a wider range of geographical and ecological environment than other animals and plants. He can often create environments favorable to himself within natural environments that are unfavorable. *Human geography* deals with man and his environmental needs, his industrial use and distribution of raw materials and the effects of natural boundaries on political boundaries and human activities. D. L. D.

SEE ALSO: AFRICA, ANTARCTICA, ASIA, AUSTRALIA, EARTH, EUROPE, NORTH AMERICA, SOIL TYPES, SOUTH AMERICA

Some invertebrates of the Middle Cambrian were trilobites and sponges

Mississippian life included many crinoids, fan-like echinoderms

All pictures Chicago Natural History Museum

The Permian sea was dotted with now-extinct mollusks and sponges

Geologic time table A most interesting and puzzling question concerning Earth is its age. As men tried to find the answer, they began to construct a time scale based on the fact that rocks, such as those in the Grand Canyon, were in layers, or *strata,* of different kinds and thicknesses. Unless they had been dislodged by earthquake or faulting, the newest layers were near the surface. Older rocks were in the lower layers. Geologists use these layers in much the same way as a calendar.

Absolute ages given in the time table have been largely verified by using chemical analyses of radioactive mineral substances. These are generally accepted by geologists, subject to a small percentage of error. In every period of geologic time, there were widespread accumulations of sedimentary strata. In fact, the strata comprise the record itself and give evidence of the climate and geographic conditions of the time, as well as containing the fossil remains of plants and animals.

Each major time unit was brought to a close by *orgeny,* or mountain building disrupting the sequence of sedimentary deposition. This uplifting or MOUNTAIN building usually ends sedimentary deposition, and exposes the rocks to erosional forces. This sequence of events is common throughout the geologic time record. The extent of this interruption varies from a short period of time to millions of years.

For convenience sake, the largest time unit is the era. In most time tables there are three eras: The PALEOZOIC ERA (700,000,000 to 230,000,000 years ago), the MESOZOIC ERA (230,000,000 to 65,000,000 years ago), and the CENOZOIC ERA (65,000,000 years ago to the present).

There is an earlier period of time that is generally called the *Precambrian* era. It is estimated that this time extends from 700,000,000 years ago back to nearly 4 billion years. The principal life forms of this time were *bacteria* and *blue-green algae.* Once this era was divided into two periods, the Archeozoic and Proterozoic. However, now we divide it into the *Early Precambrian era* and *Late Precambrian era.*

PALEOZOIC ERA

This era includes the Cambrian, Ordovician, Silurian, Devonian, Mississippian, Pennsylvanian, and Permian periods.

The greatest inundation (flood) of known geologic time occurred during the Ordovician period. Shallow seas covered a major part of the North American continent. Volcanic activity in the eastern United States spread deposits of volcanic ash over large areas. Although much of the CONTINENT was rising at the beginning of the Silurian period, seaways from the Arctic, the Gulf of Mexico, and the Gulf of California covered forty per cent of the present continent. Volcanic activity continued in the eastern United States and more than 4000 feet (1219.2 meters) of black lava was interbedded with Silurian limestones. The Silurian period on the North American continent closed with the crust of the earth in a state of quietness.

Shallow seaways moved back and forth over a small percentage of the continental area during the Devonian period. At the end of the Devonian period, emergence of

Cretaceous sea life included snails, oysters and curled ammonites

Oligocene deposits reveal the leptomeryx, a fossil deer

All pictures Chicago Natural History Museum

The northern mammoth of the Pleistocene lived in Alaska

the continent of North America was complete. Volcanoes deposited vast thicknesses of basic lava in the New England area. A disturbance called the *Acadian* came at the end of the Devonian period. This elevated a great land mass near the present eastern seaboard and formed an extensive mountain area.

During the Mississippian period, limestone deposits collected in the seaways throughout the central part of NORTH AMERICA. Uplifting was going on during the late Mississippian, probably more widespread than any previous Paleozoic era of time. This mountain building was on the eastern seaboard, in southern Arkansas, and regions of Colorado.

The Pennsylvanian time is known for its great coal formations during the Carboniferous Age. When shallow water and swampy conditions existed in the central North American continent, vegetation accumulated as peat, which eventually was transformed into COAL.

Mountain building characterized the Permian period. The Appalachian uplifting brought about great changes in the North American continent as the Paleozoic era came to an end.

MESOZOIC ERA

This era includes the Triassic, the Jurassic, and the Cretaceous periods.

Except for restricted seaways in extreme western North America, the continent was rising during most of the Triassic and Jurassic periods. Uplifting, erosion, and the depositing of red beds characterized much of the physical history of the North American continent during the Mesozoic era, and the continent began to show shorelines similar to those seen today.

CENOZOIC ERA

This era includes the Tertiary and Quaternary periods. The Tertiary period is divided into the Paleocene, Eocene, Oligocene, Miocene, and Pliocene epochs. The Quaternary period is divided into the Pleistocene and Recent epochs.

Throughout the Cenozoic eras the continental margins of North America remained similar to the ones existing today. Continental and alpine glaciation modified land forms in more than half of the continent during the Pleistocene period. There were four major continental glaciers covering Canada and northern United States. These were called the *Nebraskan,* the *Kansan,* the *Illinoian,* and the *Wisconsin.* Withdrawal of the ice sheet left the North American continent as it is seen today. These glaciers were in part responsible for the gouging out of the Great Lakes. The glaciers over the great lakes were tremendous.

The earth as it is known today is a result of many changes that have occurred during the eras, periods, and epochs of the geologic time table. This time table is like a book. A table, such as on pages 766 and 767, can help man read the history of Earth.

PALEONTOLOGY, or the identification and classification of fossil plants and animals, also fits into the geologic time table. The relative age of sedimentary rocks can be determined by the detailed study of this plant and animal evolution. These *index fossils,* as they are called, are an immense aid to historical geologists in studying earth history, because they determine specific rock age over widespread areas. A. P. M.

SEE ALSO: EARTH; EARTH, EARLY DEVELOPMENT OF; EVOLUTION; EVOLUTION OF MAN; FOSSILS; GEOLOGY; GLACIAL AGES

Age	Period	LAND FORMS	BASE OF STUDY	PLANT LIFE	ANIMAL LIFE
	PRECAMBRIAN ERA—began 4 billion years ago				
	Early Precambrian	Probably massive gas formations. Volcanic eruptions		Nothing known	Nothing known
		Volcanic activity. Mountains created and eroded to plains. Minerals deposited	Canada Scotland	Algae	Traces of unicellular marine life
	Late Precambrian	Mountains raised with extrusions of granite and gneiss. Continued volcanic eruptions, and at least two glacial periods	Grand Canyon Great Lakes	Algae	Simple marine life, worm-like bodies
	PALEOZOIC ERA—began 700 million years ago				
AGE OF INVERTEBRATES	Cambrian lasted about 100 million years	Seas swept over most of the earth. Volcanic activity and faulting created many highlands. They were eroded, the Laurentian thrust excepted	Europe Asia, Eastern Canada, Great Lakes	Algae	Brachiopods, trilobites, gastropods and sponges
AGE OF INVERTEBRATES	Ordovician lasted about 60 million years	Earth still sea-swept and level, with faulting and erosion in sequence. Volcanic activity still great. Large deposits of limestone	Canada New York	Algae	Additional marine life: foraminifera, coral, graptolites, cystoids, arachnids and nautiloids
AGE OF INVERTEBRATES	Silurian lasted about 40 million years	Great faults occurred. Appalachians raised and withstood subsequent erosion. Seas flooded inland and left great salt beds	New York Great Britain	Mosses and primitive land plants appeared	Bryozoans, crinoids, echinoids, lamellibranchs joined the invertebrate life in this era
AGE OF FISH	Devonian lasted about 50 million years	Much of present land was inundated. Upthrusts increased the Appalachian range. Pacific Coast sank. Europe and N. America connected by land bridge	New York Grand Canyon	Marine algae abundant. Ferns and lichen develop on land	First amphibians appeared. Graptolites and cystoids decreased
AGE OF AMPHIBIANS	Carboniferous Mississippian lasted 35 million years	Great floods covered Atlantic Coast and Mississippi Valley area. Lichen forests covered to form coal beds	Mississippi Valley Newfoundland	Hardy lichen covered in coal marsh. Conifers and fern trees developed	Amphibians increased. Crinoids and blastoids disappeared
AGE OF AMPHIBIANS	Pennsylvanian lasted about 40 million years	Further great floods covered Northern Europe, Asia and Pennsylvania. Coal beds are created as sphagnum and other plants are covered	Asia, Europe Pennsylvania	Warm, moist air had encouraged vegetation	Trilobites vanished and amphibians increased in size and number. Insect life increased
AGE OF AMPHIBIANS	Permian lasted about 10 million years	Volcanic activity and violent upthrusts created new mountains in U.S.A. and Europe. Swamps drained and deserts developed. Ice covered parts of earth	Texas Grand Canyon Germany	Many swamp-growing plants were lost in this era	Amphibian life began to decrease and primitive reptiles developed

	Period	Geology	Location	Plant life	Animal life
AGE OF REPTILES	**MESOZOIC ERA—began 230 million years ago**				
	Triassic lasted about 45 million years	Upthrusts and tilting violent in Germany and eastern U.S.A. Seas flooded western coast as far as Kansas. Salt beds were deposited	Germany New Jersey Nevada	Forests of conifers and cycads, ferns and fern trees grow. Air became dry, affecting vegetation	Dinosaurs and aquatic reptiles came into being
	Jurassic lasted about 45 million years	Great floods washed over the continents in both hemispheres. Land between S. America and Africa disappeared. Faulting created the Sierra Nevada range	Germany England Texas	Gymnosperms appeared. Vegetation was becoming more scant	Reptiles dominated the land, sea and air. The first bird (archaeopteryx) appeared. Modern insects, bees, moths and flies now lived
	Cretaceous lasted about 65 million years	Great beds of chalk, coal and marl are created by the most wide-spread floods on all continents. Andes and Rocky Mountains are formed	Atlantic Coast California England	Angiosperms, the first flowering plants grew. Huge conifers and other deciduous trees developed	This was the age of the tyrannosaurus and the armored, horned and duckbill primitive mammals
AGE OF MAMMALS	**CENOZOIC ERA—began 65 million years ago**				
	Tertiary				
	Paleocene and Eocene Epochs lasted about 35 million years	Gulf and Pacific Coasts are submerged. Upthrusts created wider mountain ranges in Western Hemisphere. Lands vanished in Southern Hemisphere and at South Pole	California	Seed-bearing plants and grasses were now abundant	Marsupials were in existence and grazing animals began to develop. The first carnivores were found
	Miocene lasted about 15 million years	Coasts of America rise. Volcanic activity great in U. S. A. and Europe. Andes, Alps, Himalayas and Rocky Mountains rose	Atlantic and Pacific coasts Europe (France) Asia	Modern plant life is more or less developed	The mammoth and the first horse appeared. Mammals were predominant. Anthropoid apes existed
	Pliocene lasted about 8 million years	Volcanic activity continued on Pacific Coast. Sierras and all Rocky Mt. chain increased. Appalachian range also lifted higher. Climate became cooler	California Florida Texas France		Mastodons and Old World monkeys migrated to Western Hemisphere. Carnivores and furred animals flourished
AGE OF MAN	Quaternary				
	Pleistocene lasted 6+ million years	The glacial or ice ages. The Northern Hemisphere was covered many times by ice which receded and reformed. Land bridges disappeared between the continents. Lakes and valleys were formed. Volcanic activity lessened but continued	Great Lakes Scandinavia Asia Alaska Greenland	Many plants moved with glaciers to new locations, more were destroyed	The mammoth was destroyed under ice. Man now moved into a world that was at least 4 billion years in formation
	Recent	With the receding of the ice, lakes and waterways were formed. Erosion and volcanic ash formed soil and alluvials			Neolithic man became known 20,000 years B.C.

All photos courtesy Society For Visual Education, Inc.

One of the subjects geologists study is the effects of the glaciers of thousands of years ago. This moraine valley was left by such a glacier

Geology Geology is the study of all the parts of the Earth and its history. Geologists study the ROCKS and MINERALS that make up the Earth's crust. They investigate the layers of the surface of the Earth in its rivers, valleys, and mountains to find the record or to read the story of the changing Earth.

The science of geology has found that mountains are formed in different ways. Some are made by the action of molten rock pushing up on the Earth's crust, some by the action of VOLCANOES. Still others are formed by the bending and breaking of the crust of the Earth. Even as mountains are being formed, other forces are at work wearing them down. These forces include the action of rain, wind, and GLACIERS.

The knowledge that the geologists decipher about the earth—its layers, how they were formed, and how they will probably change—is of great value today. The study of geology will tell where to search for oil, uranium, iron, copper, coal, and whatever minerals man must have for the economy of today. For example, only recently geologists have found huge deposits of iron ore in the Brazilian jungle and rich oil deposits off the shores of the United States.

There are many different kinds of specialized geologists within the general field of geology. One such specialist is the engineering geologist. He is an important member of large and heavy construction teams. Before large buildings can be constructed, it is necessary to know what type of bedrock is under the surface and how deep it extends. Test borings are taken to find this information. This type of information is also needed in the building of bridges and DAMS.

Geologists are particularly interested in understanding earthquakes and glaciers. In the Polar regions, they are measuring the thickness of snow layers, the speed at which glaciers move, and the rate and amount of melting that is taking place. Through these areas of geological research, important data will be gathered about weather and about the future level of the seas.

Glacial geologists, in studying the ice caps of the Arctic region, Greenland, and ANTARCTICA during the INTERNATIONAL GEOPHYSICAL YEAR, found that there was a great deal more glacial ice than they had thought. They found that there was about 40 percent more ice than they had estimated. They also discovered that this same ice is melting at a fairly rapid rate. More icebergs have been observed lately around the continent of Antarctica and in the region of the North Atlantic. The ice pack formed on the Arctic Ocean is becoming thinner at a measurable rate. The cause of this melting seems to lie in the fact that the mean temperature of the world is rising. This melting of glacial ice will eventually bring about a rise in sea level. It will be many, many years before all of the ice melts, if it ever does.

Little knowledge is available concerning the core of the earth. There are, of course, theories about it, but geologists are hoping that with new instruments and with each bit of knowledge they gather, they will come closer to an answer. Seismologists, working with instruments that record earthquakes, hope for a clearer record of what goes on under the earth's crust.

Seismology laboratories all over the world are continually observing movement in the earth's crust. This data on the rates of speed in which these shock waves pass through rock provides information on the earth's interior. (The rates of travel of underground shock waves differ in different types of rock. The travel time it takes for the shock wave to pass through tells the geologists the structure and composition of that particular rock layer.) Small artificial earthquakes are used to help locate petroleum and groundwater deposits.

A subject of great interest to those who study geology is the age of the earth. New developments have made it possible to date rock materials with much more certainty than ever before. New knowledge about the process by which certain elements give up their radioactivity has opened the door to the age of the past. Scientists now hope to be able to determine much more accurately the age of the earth.

Modern geologists find that they are often working with scientists from other fields. The scientists from the fields of atomic physics, chemistry, botany, MARINE BIOLOGY, meteorology, and others have a great deal to contribute. Each of these scientists, through his own field, is able to help the geologist fill in the missing links and answer many of the questions that he is otherwise unable to answer.

There are many careers in geology. If one is interested in caves, glaciers, volcanoes, FOSSILS, rock samples, or the collecting of sea shells, or even exploring for mines or oil, one may find a stimulating and rewarding career in the field of geology. V. V. N.

SEE ALSO: AFRICA, ASIA, AUSTRALIA, EARTH, EUROPE, GEOLOGIC TIME TABLE, NORTH AMERICA, PALEONTOLOGY, SEISMOGRAPH, SOUTH AMERICA

Devil's Tower is a geological phenomenon of the erosion of hard rock

Peculiar shapes have also been made in sandstone which is more easily eroded

Even small pebbles have been made smooth and round by erosion

Weathering, or erosion, can also make rounded surfaces on giant rock formations

Geometry (gee-AHM-uh-tree) Geometry is a branch of MATHEMATICS which is concerned with *forms*. It also deals with the properties and relationships of forms and figures in a plane or in space. Elementary geometry is often linked with Euclid who lived about 300 B.C., but there is evidence that it was known long before his time. The Egyptians used some of the principles to survey the land and build their temples. *Geometry,* from the Greek, means *to measure the land.* In England, the study of geometry is often referred to as the "study of Euclid." Even today in the modern world, geometry is a vital tool of measurement. It is a necessary technique for design, architecture, navigation, engineering, surveying, map-making, aeronautics, etc.

This geometry of measurement, or *metric* geometry, by itself can be no more than a collection of inferences drawn from the physical behavior of forms and figures. The principles of the physical behavior are simplified and made abstract. The abstract principles then become the basis of geometry—a science of logic and reasoning. These simplified geometry principles eliminate the inconsistencies arising with their related counterparts in the real, physical world. For example, through two chalk points, many straight lines could be drawn, depending upon the size of the points. But, as the size gets smaller and smaller, eventually the points are only an abstract concept, having no dimension—only position—then only one line can be drawn. This one line is a concept of length, abstracted from its physical relative, a chalk line.

BASIC TERMS AND ASSUMPTIONS

In building the vocabulary for the deductive science of geometry, a few, simple terms must be first agreed upon. For the basic geometry studied in school, such terms are *point, line,* and *plane*—all familiar concepts. It would be impossible to actually define these terms since they are so fundamental. Even complete descriptions of these terms involve ideas more complicated than the terms themselves. These basic terms are called *primitives.* Since geometry is a system of mathematics, valid rules of operation are necessary in manipulating these primitives, such as connecting one point to another, or finding the point where two lines intersect.

The primitives are groundwork for more technical vocabulary. Next, the basic definitions are stated in terms of the primitives, as are also the axioms and postulates. *Axioms* and *postulates* are the simplified abstracted principles mentioned above. They are statements assumed to be *true without proof.* In order to have a practical, workable geometry in the everyday field of measurement, it is necessary that the axioms and postulates correspond well with the physical objects and their properties. Only after extensive observations and testing are these assumptions admitted to the system.

In geometry, then, the primitives, basic definitions, and assumptions, or statements of evident truths, form the foundation for the system. All these are regarded as true and are not questioned further within the framework of the system. From these truths are derived statements and conclusions concerning properties and relationships of geometric figures. Each statement or conclusion so derived or proved is in turn used to assist in proving more statements until a large set of conclusions is built. From these come a large structure of geometric principles, each of which in turn depends upon something previously proved.

To prove the truth of various geometric facts, logical and systematic reasoning is necessary. Seeing, in geometry, is not believing. The evidence of one's eyes is not always trustworthy. Although observation and experiment play a large role in the study of geometry, a conclusion cannot be based upon these sources alone. Final decisions must rest on proof. The conclusions reached are of great importance, yet the kind of thinking or reasoning used in reaching the conclusions is equally important.

Although several types of reasoning exist, the one most common to the geometric proof is *deductive reasoning.* Deductive reasoning starts from a general principle or truth already established by definition, by assumption, or by previous reasoning. Usually, a condition is stated for a certain class.

COMMON GEOMETRIC FIGURES

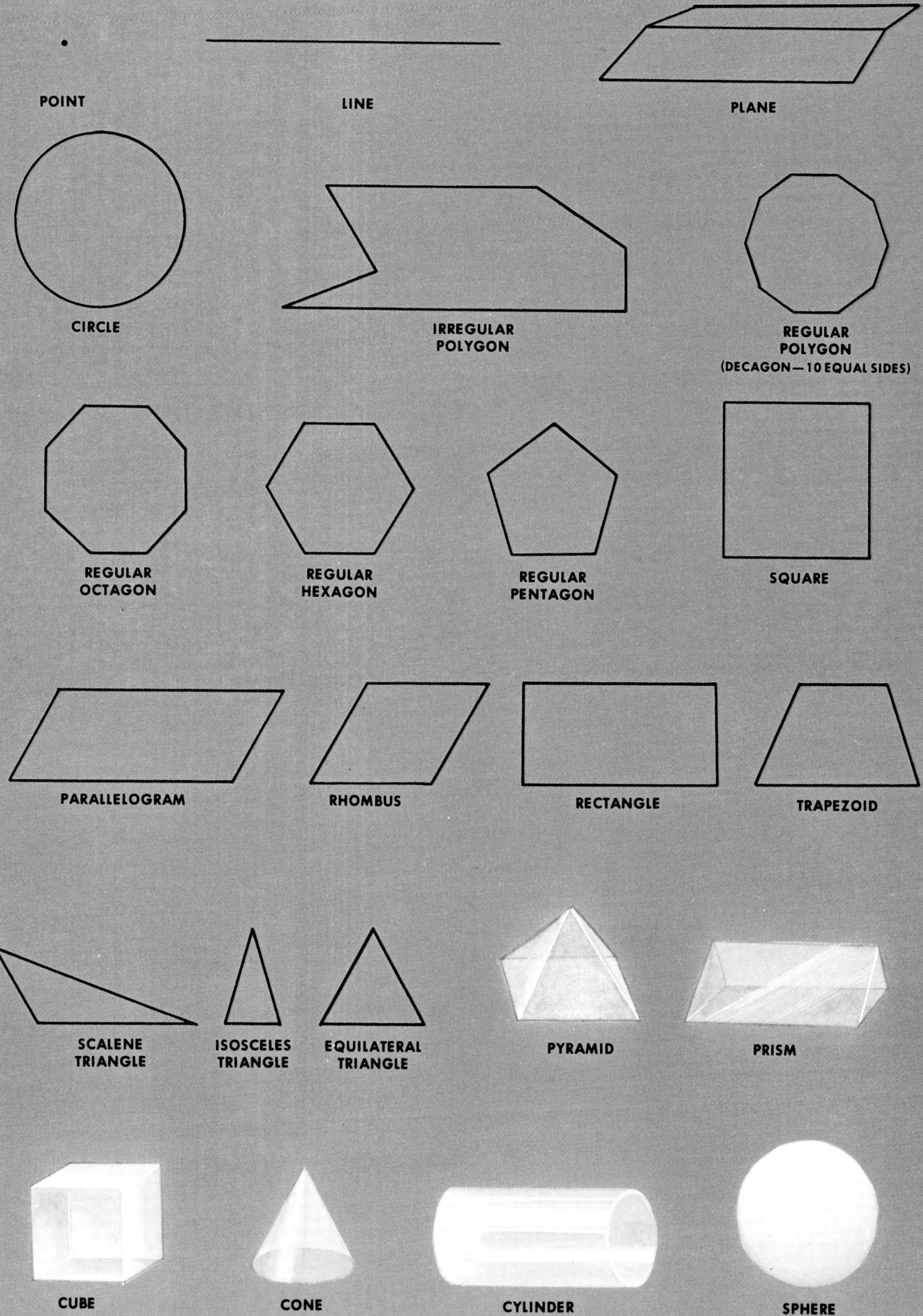

The next step is to show that a particular case in mind belongs to that certain class. The conclusion may then be drawn: the condition which applied to the general class must apply to the particular case placed in the general class.

An example of general deductive reasoning is the following:

All animals that have lungs, body scales, and a backbone are reptiles.

My pet has lungs, body scales, and a backbone.

Therefore, my pet is a reptile.

The same type of reasoning applied to geometry is the following:

The diameter of a circle is twice the length of the radius. (This is an axiom.)

The radius of this circle is two inches.

Therefore, the diameter is four inches.

TYPES OF GEOMETRY

Many classifications of geometry exist. One grouping describes the type of transformation allowed. The familiar *elementary Euclidean geometry,* plane and solid, was named in honor of a famous mathematician whose geometry with only slight modifications is still in use today. This kind deals with rigid transformations—so that lengths, measure of angles, areas and volumes do not alter under transformation. *Projective* geometry deals with the properties of figures recognizable after distortion by projection. Drastic transformations lead to a branch called *topology.*

Other classifications include *analytic* geometry, which uses algebraic equations and a coordinate system to describe geometric relationships. *Differential* geometry covers the properties of curves and surfaces in a three dimensional Euclidean space.

Non-Euclidean geometry can be any type of geometry which alters an assumption of Euclid's. This Euclidean postulate, modified by Playfair, "Through a given point not on a given line, one and only one straight line can be drawn parallel to the given line" is a favorite "weak" spot attacked by non-Euclidean geometers. Many feel that this postulate is weak because it is impossible to know what will happen to the lines at an infinite distance, and it is the only Euclidean assumption depending to such a large extent upon imagination. *Hyperbolic* geometry suggests that there can be several lines parallel to a given line through a given point not on the given line. *Elliptic* geometry claims that parallel lines will intersect if extended far enough. Both these non-Euclidean geometries have applications in science and are valuable modern contributions. It was in elliptic geometry that EINSTEIN stated his theory of relativity. D. L. D.

SEE ALSO: ALGEBRA

Geophysics The science of geophysics studies the physical properties of the earth, and deals with such subjects as WEATHER, EARTHQUAKES, TIDES, and GRAVITY. It is especially concerned with forces which cannot be observed directly, and must be recorded with sensitive instruments.

SEE: EARTH, GEOLOGY

Geothermal energy Geothermal energy is the energy produced by releasing steam and hot water from natural hot areas in the earth's crust by use of drill holes. Its main uses are for heating and for generating ELECTRICITY.

Geothermal energy has been used in Italy since 1905; in Iceland since 1925; and in northern California since 1960. With limited supplies of FOSSIL FUELS, it could become an important energy source. Geothermal energy is inexpensive and non-polluting. However, it is hard to transport, it gives off foul-smelling gases, and it can only be tapped in rare volcanic areas or HOT SPRINGS. P.P.S.

SEE ALSO: ENERGY, GEYSERS

Geotropism see Tropism

Geranium Geranium plants have large red, pink, or white blossoms. Several simple flowers grow in a cluster on one stalk. The leaves are heart-shaped and some are heavily scented. Leaves may be used to flavor jellies and to make perfumes. Geraniums need a large amount of sun, but too much water will injure their growth.

The geranium plant originally came from Africa and Australia.

Geriatrics see Aging

Germ Though the word "germ" is sometimes used to mean "seed," or particle from which an organism can grow, it is usually used to mean any of the tiny organisms which cause disease.

SEE: PATHOLOGY

Germ layer theory see Embryology; Heredity; Weismann, August

Germ theory The germ theory of disease states that DISEASE is caused by living germs which enter the body. These germs can be spread by contact with an infected person, by articles touched by the person, or by air. Germs are any BACTERIA, fungi, viruses, or one-celled animals which cause disease. They usually can be seen only with a MICROSCOPE. This theory of disease is accepted throughout the world today.

This was not always true, for long ago people had many theories as to the cause of sickness. Some thought disease was sent by the gods to punish men. Others thought that disease was caused by "bad" air or "bad" blood, or by demons which captured a man's body.

In 1676 ANTONY VAN LEEUWENHOEK invented the microscope which made it possible to see germs. In 1825 Agostino Bassi discovered that bacteria caused a disease in silkworms. LOUIS PASTEUR, 35 years later, discovered a cure for the disease by killing the bacteria. He then stated the germ theory as it is known today. ROBERT KOCH, in 1876, proved that bacteria caused anthrax in cattle. In 1860, JOSEPH LISTER discovered that killing the bacteria in a surgical wound stopped the infections that frequently occurred after surgery.

It was many years before people generally accepted the germ theory. The early scientists were hampered in proving it because they were not allowed to use live animals in their experiments. However, this germ theory was the beginning of modern medical control of disease. J. K. L.

SEE ALSO: BACTERIOLOGY, FUNGUS, MEDICINE, PATHOLOGY, PROTOZOA, VIRUS

Germanium (jer-MAY-nee-um) Germanium is a silvery-gray, hard, brittle metal. It is found in zinc ores and in large amounts in the mineral *germanite*. Clemens A. Winkler, a German, separated pure germanium for the first time in 1886. He did this by melting *argyrodite*, a rare silver ore containing germanium oxide, and passing hydrogen gas over it. He named the new ELEMENT *germanium* in honor of Germany. Germanium (symbol Ge) is element number 32. Its atomic weight is 72.59. Chemically, it is a METAL and so it does not react with solutions of acids and bases as nonmetals do.

Germanium has an important use as the main ingredient in TRANSISTORS. Transistors are used in place of VACUUM TUBES in radios, computers, and other communication devices. They are preferable to tubes because they are much smaller, use less ENERGY, do not get hot, and last about ten years. Transistors are made of a germanium crystal and a very small amount of arsenic or GALLIUM. The germanium in the transistor is one of the purest forms of any material that exists. The three inner shells of a germanium atom are filled and the outer shell holds four electrons. Covalent bonds fill the shell to eight electrons. When arsenic or gallium is added, the crystal bond has one too many or one too few electrons. This imbalance allows electricity to pass through the crystal in one direction. J. K. L.

SEE ALSO: CRYSTAL, ELEMENTS

Shared electrons let current pass in germanium

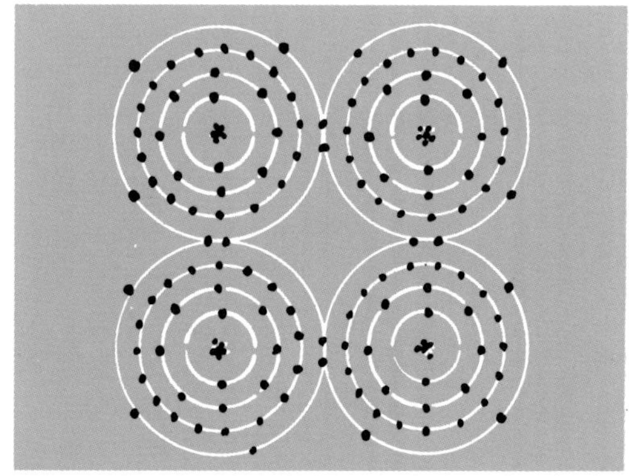

✳ THINGS TO DO

DO SEEDS ALWAYS GROW IN THE SAME DIRECTION?

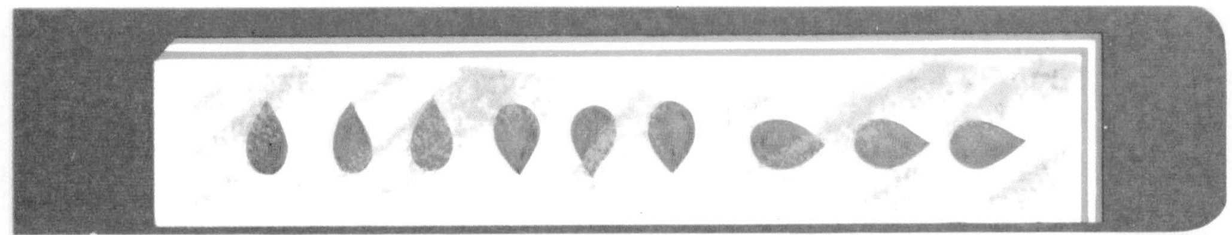

1. **Make a glass sandwich as described below.**
2. **Select one kind of seed; e.g. sunflower seeds. Place three seeds each with the pointed end up, the rounded end up, and on their sides.**
3. **Observe the direction of growth of each minute plant as it germinates. Can you see a pattern? Why does this occur?**

✳ THINGS TO DO

DO ALL SEEDS GERMINATE AT THE SAME RATE?

1. **Select a variety of seeds: radish, corn, bean, sunflower, apple, and acorn.**
2. **Soak all the seeds overnight to help loosen their seed coats.**
3. **Make a long glass sandwich with a cotton layer between. Place the seeds in a row along one side.**
4. **Tie the sandwich together and stand it upright in a cake pan of water.**
5. **Watch it daily for the first signs of germination. Which seeds sprouted first? Which ones took the longest time?**

Germination Germination is the growth and development of an embryo into a young plant. It starts in the seed when temperature, water, and oxygen conditions are right and is over when the plant is able to make food.

SEE: PLANT, PROPAGATION, SEED

Gestation period (jess-TAY-shuhn) Most female mammals carry their young insidc their bodies for many days. This is called *gestation* or *pregnancy*. It begins when the egg is fertilized and ends with birth.

The gestation period varies according to the species of mammal. In general, the length of time is in proportion to the size of the adult. While pregnancy for an elephant is 21 months, young hamsters are born in only 16 days. On the other hand, since pouched mammals, *marsupials,* nurture their young in a pouch, the young are born only partially developed. Gestation time for the large kangaroo is only 39 days. E. P. L.

SEE ALSO: EMBRYOLOGY, MAMMALIA

AVERAGE GESTATION PERIODS (in days)

Animal	Days	Animal	Days
HAMSTER	16	TIGER	112
MOUSE	19-21	SHEEP	145-150
RAT	20-22	MONKEY	188
RABBIT	30-32	APE	209
KANGAROO	39	BEAR	210
FOX	52-62	MAN	265-270
CAT	55-63	COW	270-284
DOG	61-63	HORSE	330-337
GUINEA PIG	66-68	WHALE	360-370
LION	105-108	CAMEL	400
PIG	100-110	ELEPHANT	600-655

Geyser (GYE-zer) Geysers are hot springs that throw hot water and steam high into the air. A geyser does not erupt all of the time but boils up from time to time. A few are very regular in the time that they erupt. Geysers are found only in a few parts of the world.

Geysers erupt from small shallow pools of heated water and cause great columns of water and steam to be ejected high into the air. These *geyser pools* are fed by a narrow tube that extends far down into the earth where water becomes heated. A mineral deposit called *geyserite* is formed around both HOT SPRINGS and geysers. Often this deposit is colored by algae that lives in the hot springs.

A geyser is produced as groundwater is heated by subsurface volcanic activity. Often this water is heated well above its normal boiling point of 212° F. (100° C.). This is possible due to the weight of the water in the tube which, in turn, places great pressure on the water in the area of heating. When the water is heated enough to overcome this pressure, the geyser erupts and the whole process begins again. Old Faithful in Yellowstone National Park, Wyoming is a famous geyser. H.S.G.

Giant Giants are very tall people, over 8 feet (2.4 meters) high. There is a gland near the brain which makes a substanced called a growth HORMONE. If too much of the hormone is put into the blood of children under 12 to 14 years old, they become giants.

In spite of their great height, these giants are normally proportioned. In early years, they are strong and intelligent. Later, when the PITUITARY GLAND becomes less active, they can become weak and mentally slower.

The great increase in size in giantism is due to over-secretion before bone-forming centers have stopped functioning. If an over-secretion of growth hormone occurs in adulthood after the bones have stopped growing, a condition known as ACROMEGALY develops. Bones of the hands, feet, and face become enlarged and out of proportion. There is no increase in height.

The growth hormone, known as *somato-*

Courtesy Society For Visual Education, Inc.

Pressure sends the water high into the air

tropin or STH, has many actions rather than a single action on one particular endocrine gland. It seems to increase the effectiveness of several other hormones. Such an action is called *synergistic*. For example, when the ovaries and pituitary gland in a rat are removed, the milk glands become inactive. If either the female hormone, *estrogen*, or the growth hormone are injected, milk glands are not reactivated. However, if the two hormones are used together, milk glands become active. The growth hormone enables estrogen to exert its full effect. It has no effect if used alone on the thyroid, sex organs, or the adrenal cortex (outer part). If used with the pituitary hormones that act on these glands, their effectiveness is increased. J. C. K.

SEE ALSO: MIDGET

Giant star see Stars

Giauque, William F. (1895-1982) William Giauque won the 1949 NOBEL PRIZE in chemistry. His important research in the field of *cryogenics* studied what happened to matter at the lowest temperatures ever reached. He discovered two new ISOTOPES of OXYGEN.

In studying the effects of extremely low temperatures on the properties of matter, Giauque succeeded in reaching temperatures as low as a fraction of a degree above ABSOLUTE ZERO. His studies have contributed much to chemical THERMODYNAMICS. The methods he used in the discovery of oxygen 17 and 18 were adopted by other scientists, who discovered the isotope *deuterium*. In industry Giauque's experiments have led to important techniques for producing petroleum and rubber products, cheaper fertilizers, and other products. A.J.H.

Chicago Natural History Museum

Gibbon The gibbon is the smallest of the anthropoid apes. It lives in Southeast Asia and in the East Indies. Gibbons have long arms, short legs, and seldom grow more than 3 feet (.9 meter) tall. When they stand erect their arms can touch the ground. Of all apes gibbons spend the most time in trees. Although they prefer life in the trees, they can walk erect when they do come to the ground. The gibbon is the only one of the APES that can do this without discomfort and without the need for some kind of support.

Considered the acrobats of the apes, gibbons swing gracefully and swiftly from branch to branch as they travel through the jungle. As they swing with their arms, they often carry food with their legs. The gibbon can use both feet and hands for grasping and handling objects. This is possible because of the presence of a "thumb" on both hands and feet.

Gibbons do not build nests in trees. They sleep on branches instead. They travel together in a family group which consists of mother, father, and children. They may live in the forests for 20 to 30 years, but in captivity their lifespan is much shorter.

Gibbons are shy, timid animals, but when cornered or attacked they will fight fiercely. Gibbons can be tamed easily and make very affectionate pets. They eat leaves, nuts, fruits, birds, eggs, and spiders.

Gibbons make a whooping sound as they communicate with each other. They have "sitting callosities," a thickened, swollen protuberance on the buttocks.

The female gibbon gives birth to one baby at a time. Two of the most common types of gibbons are the white-handed gibbon, which is the smaller variety, and the Sumatran Siamang, which tends to be larger. G. A. D.

Gibbs, Josiah Willard (1839-1903) Josiah Gibbs was the most outstanding mathematical physicist of his day. He laid the foundation for physical chemistry. The research he conducted in physical chemistry, metallurgy, and electrochemistry resulted in improved methods of manufacturing. He also was responsible for many advances that were made in medicine, biology, and physiology.

Born in New Haven, Connecticut, Gibbs graduated from Yale University in 1858 and in 1863 went to Europe to study at the universities of Paris, Berlin, and Heidelberg. When he returned to New Haven, he was appointed professor of mathematical physics at Yale, a position he held until his death on April 28, 1903.

Professor Gibbs wrote a number of famous papers, many of which were translated into German and French. Through these he became known at home and abroad. He was awarded the Copley Medal by the Royal Society of London because he was "the first to apply the second law of THERMODYNAMICS to the exhaustive discussion of the relation between chemical, electrical, and thermal energy and capacity for external work." D. H. J.

Gila monster (HEE-luh) The Gila monster is a sluggish, two-foot (.61-meter) long lizard found in the southwestern part of the United States. It is the only poisonous lizard in the New World. It must bite to inject its poison.

The body is thick, the tail short and rounded. Small, bead-shaped scales cover the body surface. Head and body are colored with black and either coral, light pink, or yellow. When the skin is shed, it comes off in pieces. The inside of the mouth is black and teeth

Gila monster
Courtesy Society For Visual Education, Inc.

are grooved to provide channels for the flow of poisonous saliva. It probably feeds on eggs and small rodents. Food is stored for future use as tail fat.

They bury 6 to 13 large, soft-shelled eggs in sand near a stream, giving them no care.

J. C. K.

SEE ALSO: REPTILIA

Gilbert, Grove Karl (1843-1918) Grove Gilbert was an American geologist who identified and described ancient Lake Bonneville from fossil and geologic evidence.

Two years later Gilbert began a three-year survey of the lower canyons of the Colorado River by boat, of Central Arizona by pack train, and again of the Colorado by boat to the Gulf of California. As a result, he published two papers in which he discussed the basin range and plateau provinces. He also named and described ancient Lake Bonneville.

After serving as a senior geologist of the United States geological survey in Utah, Gilbert became head geologist of the Appalachian Division of Geology. In 1899 he gave up most of his administrative duties to return to his study of Colorado, Mexico, and Alaska. Fortunately, he was able to accompany the Harriman Expedition to Alaska. However, his greatest contribution to geology remains the identification of Lake Bonneville.

D. H. J.

Gill Gills are organs of breathing used by most fishes and certain other lungless animals.

Gills are constructed of numerous thin layers of tissue, protected in most fish by gill covers. (Sharks and lampreys have simple round openings.) Water taken in through the mouth is forced past the membranes. Numerous blood vessels absorb oxygen, and give off carbon dioxide. The gaseous exchange process is similar to that which occurs in lungs.

Clams, crayfish and related animals also use gill-like organs.

The thin ridges seen on the underside of MUSHROOM caps are also called gills. They contain spores (reproductive cells) and are not related to respiration.

D. J. I.

SEE ALSO: LUNG, RESPIRATORY SYSTEM

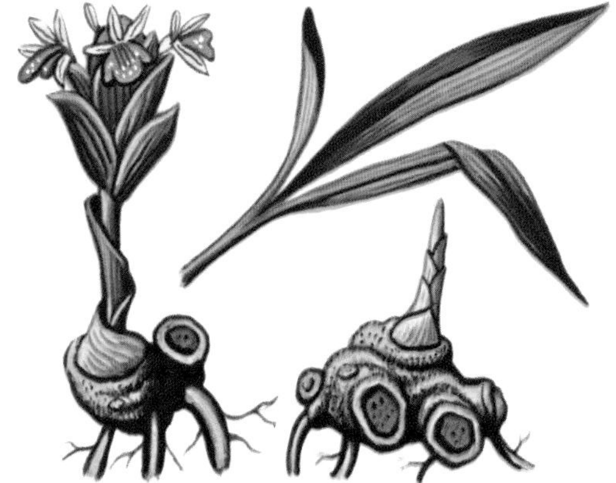

Ginger

Ginger Ginger is an important spice that is obtained from dried underground stems (*rhizomes*). It was used hundreds of years ago in the Orient and was one of the first oriental spices to be known in Europe. In cooking, ginger is often used to flavor soups, pudding, pickles, gingerbread, cookies, and beverages such as ginger ale.

The ginger plant is a perennial HERB. Its roots grow from RHIZOMES. The ginger is obtained from processing the rhizomes. The root is scraped and ground to get powdered ginger. The ginger plant grows 3 to 4 feet (.91 to 1.22 meters) tall and has bright green leaves and clusters of yellowish-green flowers with purple lips and yellow spots. Its FRUIT is a hard, dry CAPSULE. It is raised chiefly in China, Japan, and Jamaica and other Caribbean islands. Ginger needs higher temperatures than those found in the United States.

M.R.L.

The mudpuppy (top left) has ear-like external gills. The true fish (top right) has inner gills and gill covers. The crayfish's gills (bottom) are covered by the carapace

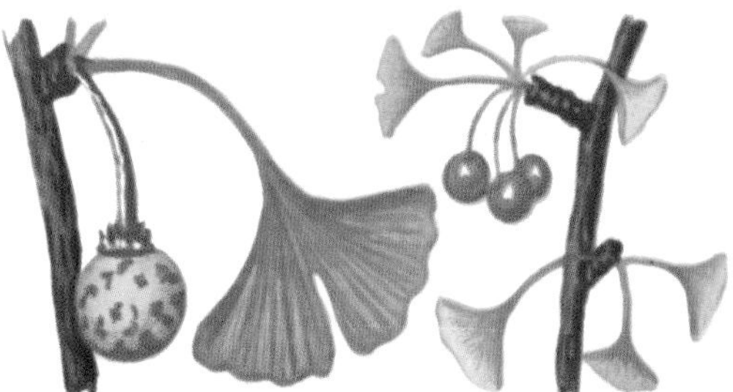

Ginkgo tree, leaf and fruit

Ginkgo (GING-koh) The ginkgo is a tall slender tree native to the Orient where it is a sacred tree planted near temples. In America and Europe it is planted for shade and ornament. It has never been found growing wild. It is sometimes called the *maidenhair* tree.

The Ginkgo *biloba* is called a living fossil because it apparently is identical with fossils dating back 75,000,000 years. It is the only surviving example of a group of trees living in ancient times.

Ginkgo, along with the conifers (pine, fir, cedar), belongs in the *gymnospermae,* a group characterized by cones and needle or fern-like leaves. Ginkgo is not evergreen and its leaves are fan-shaped with veins (venation) resembling that of the maidenhair fern. The trees are *dioecious* (separate male plants and female plants) with ovule-bearing stalks on the female trees and pollen cones on the male. The fleshy hard-centered seeds develop an unpleasant odor after falling to the ground. E. M. S.

SEE ALSO: GYMNOSPERMS

Ginseng Ginseng is a low-growing, sweet-smelling, perennial HERB with thick roots. The true ginseng of east Asia was once thought to have power to cure almost all diseases.

The ginseng plant and its odd-shaped root

Giraffe The giraffe grows to be the tallest animal in the world. It is also one of the most quiet. A giraffe is a mute, which means that it does not have a voice. Some people think it can make small sounds. Because its full height of 18 feet (5.49 meters) makes it too tall to travel, only very young giraffes can be brought to zoos from their native Africa.

Its long neck, protruding lower lip, and eighteen-inch (45.72-centimeter) tongue permit the giraffe to reach and eat the leaves of tall trees. This neck, although long, has the same number of vertebrae as found in whales, mice, and most other mammals. Even when resting, with legs folded under its body, it extends its head and neck watchfully. To eat or drink from the ground, the giraffe must balance its body by side-stretching its forelegs.

Giraffes live in herds with five to forty others. Their blotchy coloring acts as CAMOUFLAGE against trees. The hair is smooth and short with a stubby mane down neck and back. The name *giraffe* means "to walk slowly" but they can outrun most horses. Kicking with hoofed feet also gives some protection, but when finally cornered they offer little or no resistance.

An *okapi* is a giraffe with a much smaller and shorter neck. J. A. D.

Chicago Natural History Museum

Giraffes

Gizzard The gizzard is the second stomach of birds. It contains gravel which grinds up the partially digested food from the first stomach by the action of muscular walls.

SEE: BIRD, DIGESTIVE SYSTEM

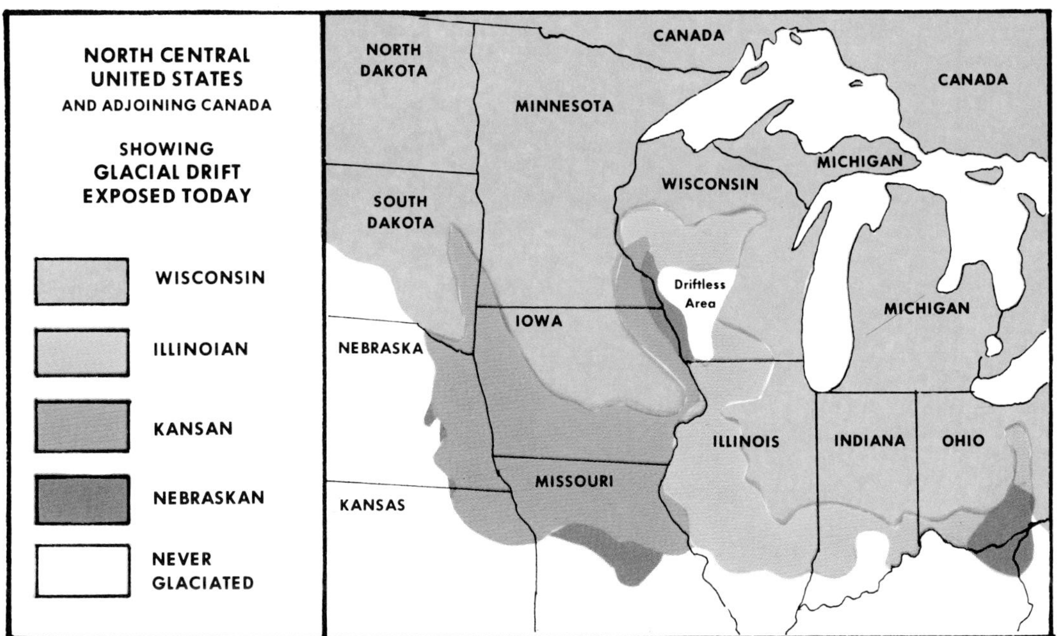

Glacial ages In the history of the earth, there were several times when much of the earth's surface was covered with ice. These different periods make up the glacial ages.

Geologists have divided the earth's history into four major periods of time, or *eras.* These eras are subdivided according to certain changes and events, into *epochs.* The *Pleistocene Epoch* is in the most recent era and is the time of the glacial ages.

There were four main stages of continental glaciation during the Pleistocene epoch, as well as substages. During the height of each stage, large portions of North America, Europe, and Asia were covered by ice. Between these stages the ice retreated to the Arctic region and the climate became warmer. The cycle was then repeated.

Glacial geologists estimate that the great continental glaciers and the Pleistocene epoch began about one million years ago. In North America the four main stages of glaciation have been named for the southernmost region that they covered. The first stage was the *Nebraskan* followed by the *Kansan.* Next came the *Illinoisan,* and last and most recent, the *Wisconsin.* The Wisconsin stage advanced to a point just to the east and south of Springfield, Illinois, where it then started to retreat 11,000 years ago. Many geologists feel that we are now in an interglacial stage and that, in time, glacial ice will again cover parts of North America.

The four glacial ages often go by their European names which are, in order of time, the *Würm, Riss, Mindel,* and *Günz.*

At the beginning of each glacial age, the summers grew cool and the sheets of ice moved south. In North America they covered much of Canada, most of the upper Mississippi River Valley, and the northeast part of the country north of the Ohio River. As the ice moved south the animals also moved south where it was warmer, though some were caught in the ice and preserved. Then the summers became warmer as the ice left and the animals moved back north again.

In North America there are three main areas that seem to be the centers from which the glacial ice spread. These areas or centers have been named for their location. The *Labradorean center* is in the middle of the Labrador Plateau. Ice came as far west as the Missouri River from the *Keewatin* center in central Canada. The third center is the *Cordilleran center.* This glacier came from far western Canada and moved down into Washington and Oregon.

As the glaciers advanced, they picked up all kinds of rock debris and soil. When the glacier started to melt and retreat, this material was deposited in a type of landform termed MORAINE. The glaciers are responsible for much of the landforms and topography of north central North America. The Great Lakes and Niagara Falls, as well as many of the major river systems, are the result of continental glaciation. H. S. G.

SEE ALSO: CENOZOIC ERA, GEOLOGIC TIME TABLE

Courtesy Society For Visual Education, Inc.

Ice of valley glaciers is usually thick. Crevasses form as it moves over rough ground

Courtesy Society For Visual Education, Inc.

Glacier Some areas of the earth are covered by ice layers. These layers are found in very high mountains and around the North and South poles.

There are three basic types of glaciers. The great ice sheets that once covered most of the continents are called *continental* glaciers. The "rivers" of ice that are found in very high mountain valleys are termed *alpine* or *valley* glaciers. When two valley glaciers unite on a flat plain, it then becomes a *Piedmont* glacier.

Glacial ice will form in any area that receives more snow than will melt in the course of a year. The snow that does not quite melt builds up over the years into a granular icelike material called *firn* or *névé*. As the thickness of the névé becomes greater, it slowly turns into true glacial ice. As these deposits of ice become greater, they begin to flow and move as the result of gravity and the great pressures within the ice. It is also believed that glaciers move due to the melting and refreezing that takes place at the bottom of the ice. As glaciers move, they pluck up and carry much rock material and deposit it as they stop, melt, and recede. H.S.G.

Gladiolus Gladiolus is any of several hundred kinds of garden flowers of the IRIS family. The cone-shaped flowers occur in many colors along one side of a stiff stem. The ones near the base of the stem open first.

Gladioli, native to southern Africa, have been *hybridized,* or cross-bred, into numerous varieties. Improved characteristics have made them standard ornamental garden flowers. They are often called "glads."

They grow from an underground stem called a CORM. This part is delicate and cannot stand freezing temperatures. When corms are planted in spring, new little ones develop from the old ones which shrivel and die. So, unlike a bulb, a single corm produces only a single blossoming plant. J. F. B.

White gladiolus in bloom

Gland In animals, a gland is one or more cells specialized for the making of secretions which are of use to the organism.

SEE: ANIMAL; ENDOCRINE GLANDS; GLANDULAR TISSUE; HORMONES, PLANT; OIL GLAND; PLANT; SALIVARY GLAND

Glanders see Animal diseases

Glandular fever see Mononucleosis

Glandular tissue Glandular tissue is made of masses of body cells that form secretions, substances for use in the body. Secretion of glands such as LIVER, PANCREAS, and salivary glands aid in digestion, while tear glands and SWEAT GLANDS keep eyes and skin moist. Glands which empty their secretions through ducts are called glands of external secretion, or *exocrine* glands. The *endocrine* glands have no ducts but put their secretions directly into the bloodstream.

The secretions from the ductless glands, called hormones, are carried through the body by the blood stream or lymph. The THYROID, PITUITARY, THYMUS, adrenal, ovaries, testes, and parts of the pancreas are glands that produce hormones necessary to life. Glands are usually outgrowths of EPITHELIAL TISSUE. E. M. S.

SEE ALSO: ADRENAL GLANDS, CELL, CIRCULATORY SYSTEM, HISTOLOGY

Glaser, Donald (1926-) Donald A. Glaser received the 1960 NOBEL PRIZE in physics. Glaser invented the *bubble chamber* in 1952. The bubble chamber is a device used to track speeding atomic particles. It allows scientists to photograph the trails of atomic particles. Many new atomic particles were discovered with it.

Glaser's bubble chamber has replaced the Wilson cloud chamber in many atomic research laboratories. It is a faster and more accurate means of providing information about atomic particles. The small device is placed in the path of accelerated atoms. It uses a liquid under pressure. Speeding particles produce a trail of bubbles that are rapidly photographed. Glaser has also researched molecular biology and microbiology. A.J.H.

Glass Glass is a natural and man-made product. It is made largely of silica, limestone, and soda ash. It also may contain small portions of almost every inorganic chemical. Glass is used in windows, containers, light bulbs, automobiles, planes and thousands of other items.

Glass is usually thought of as a shiny substance that can be seen through and which breaks easily. Ordinary glass does this but glass today is made strong enough to hammer a nail into wood, resist acids, and stop bullets. There are over 50,000 kinds of glass made for different purposes.

The formula for a common kind of glass, *soda-lime* glass, is 72% white sand, 15% soda, 9% lime, 3½% aluminum oxide, and about ½% of boric acid. This glass is used in making tubing for beginner's chemistry sets. It melts at the relatively low temperature of 1350° F. (732.2° C.).

According to one legend, glass was discovered around 5000 B.C. by a group of Phoenecian sailors who, by chance, used blocks of soda to hold up their cooking pot. The intense heat melted the soda and the sand and thereby produced the first glass. Actually, volcanic fires produced natural glass (*obsidian*) long before man.

The earliest-known glass-making was in ancient Egypt, about the 16th century B.C. The process was crude, laborious and expensive. Only rich people could afford glass objects. This was true until the fourth century A.D. when the glass *blow-pipe* was invented.

The first skilled glass workers appeared during the Roman Empire. They made glass that was clear, and they also learned to make colored and decorated glass.

By the late 13th century, a Venetian guild of glass workers had formed. They perfected the now-famous Cristallo glass, a very clear kind. It could be blown into new and elaborate forms.

American colonial glass-making started in Jamestown as early as 1609. These early ventures failed for lack of skilled craftsmen, and for the next hundred years American industry made little progress. By the time of the American Revolution, several good but still high-cost glass plants were flourishing, particularly in eastern Pennsylvania. After the 1890's, many modern glass works were active in the United States and specialized glass plants are very important today.

Glass has certain characteristics not found in other materials. It is nonporous and nonabsorptive and, therefore, it is resistant to many substances, including acids. It is a good dielectric and is one of the best electrical

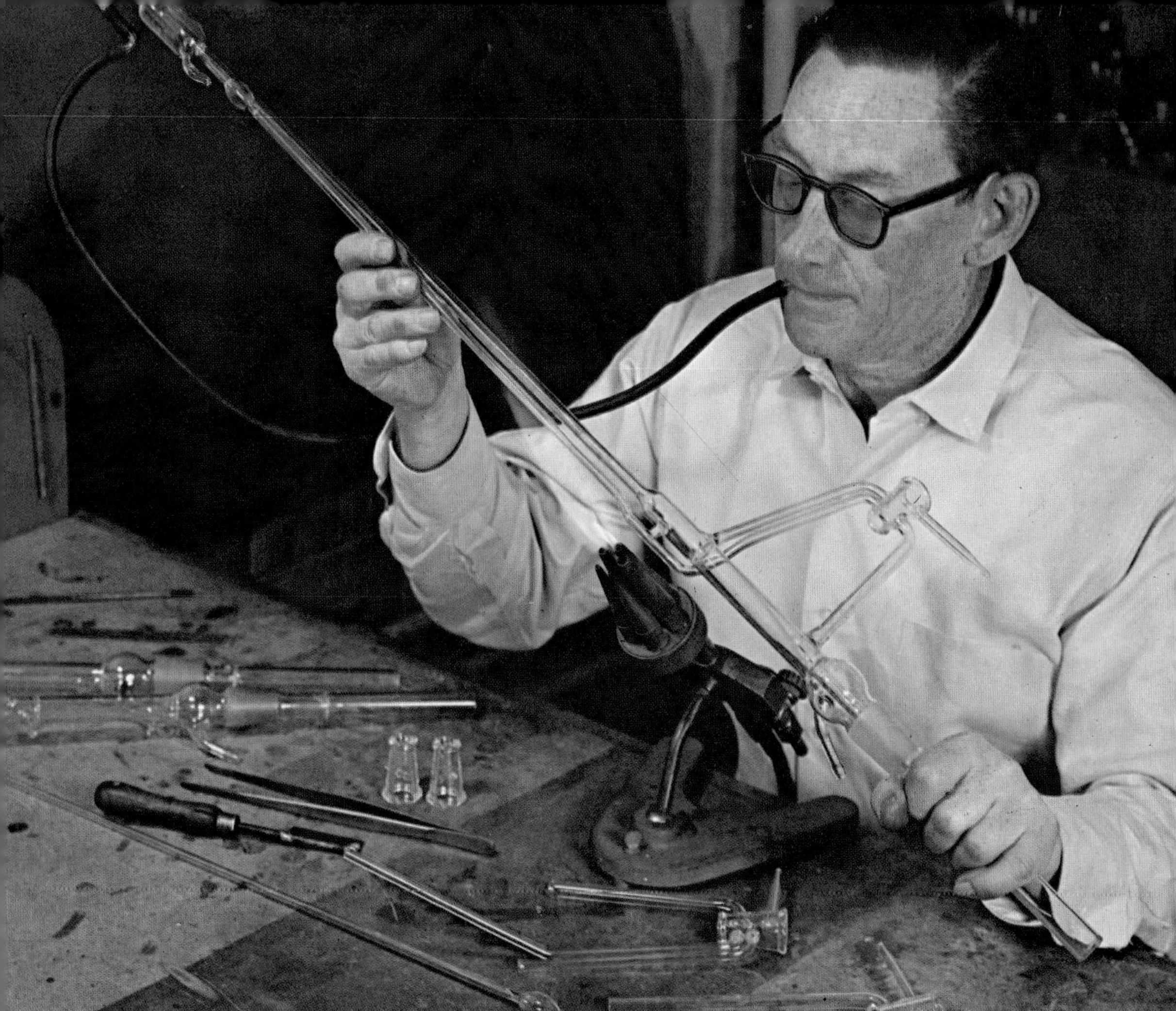

Delicate technical glass instruments are handblown by skilled technicians Kimble Glass Co.

insulators. Glass has a low thermal (heat) conductivity and a very low coefficient of expansion. It is used where materials need to be heated. Glass is high in compression strength and can withstand 80,000 to 150,000 pounds pressure per square inch (about 200,000 to 372,000 grams per square centimeter).

Glass can be made in many ways. It can be hand-molded, cast, blown, and rolled. Other methods involve drawing processes which produce sheet glass, tubing, and rolled glass. Glass today is made for every purpose in industry and the home, but the most common type made is decorative glass which involves grinding, sandblasting, etching, and enameling of glass. Safety glass includes laminated and heat-treated glass. Glass fiber and glass wool were discovered years ago. Glass fiber and spun glass are coming into use for fireproof curtains and insulating fabrics. E. Y. K.

Glasses see Lens, man-made

Glaucoma Glaucoma is an eye disease which can cause blindness. When a person looks at his EYE in a mirror, he first sees a round spot of color, such as blue. This is the *iris*. What he may not see is the transparent *cornea,* a layer that protects the eye. Between the cornea and the lens is a layer of clear fluid, called *aqueous humor*.

New fluid is always being formed, and tiny canals at the edge of the iris carry away old fluid. With glaucoma, the canals are blocked. Fluid collects and damages the eyeball.

Accumulation of this fluid creates pressure and results in hardening of the eye tissue. In acute cases, in which sight may disappear in a few hours, removal of a portion of the iris gives drainage space and usually restores sight. In chronic cases, drugs are used which cause the pupil to contract. The base of the iris is pulled away from the cornea and the fluid can drain. E. P. L.

Glenn, John H. see Space travel

Gliding joint see Joints, skeletal

Globe A globe is a ball-shaped model showing the EARTH or the sky. Because of its curvature, the surface of the earth can only be shown accurately with a terrestial globe.

SEE: MAP-MAKING

Globulin A globulin is a PROTEIN soluble in weak solutions of neutral salts but not in water. Gamma globulin in SERUM is an ANTIBODY protein.

SEE: BLOOD

Glomar Challenger The Glomar Challenger is an oceanographic research vessel. It is currently used in the *Deep Sea Drilling Project.* It was designed to make drillings and take *core samples* of the ocean bottom. This information helps scientists better understand the CONTINENTAL DRIFT.

In 1968 the Glomar Challenger began a series of cruises carrying an international team of scientists. This ship is equipped with a drilling derrick that is capable of working to a maximum depth of 6,245 meters (20,488.85 feet) of water, and can penetrate 1,300 meters (4265.09 feet) of rock beneath the ocean.

The Glomar Challenger is a remarkable ship because it can maintain a constant position over the drill site. This enables the scientists to drill in open ocean. This ship is capable of leaving a drill site and later returning to the precise spot to re-enter its original hole in the earth's crust. P.P.S.

SEE ALSO: INTERNATIONAL OCEANOGRAPHIC DECADE, OCEANOGRAPHY

Gloxinia (glock-SIN-ee-uh) Gloxinia is a plant with large bell-shaped flowers. The blossoms are red, purple, blue, or white, and the soft, velvety leaves of the plant are richly colored.

Gloxinias first grew in Brazil, but they

Gloxinia F. A. Blashfield

can be grown with care in the garden. They make excellent house plants for sunny windows, but they need a moist atmosphere.

They are best grown from seed, but excellent varieties can be obtained by planting cuttings of medium-sized leaves to which a small part of the stem is attached. After blooming they need a rest period. P.G.B.

Glucose see Sugar

Glutelin Glutelin is a simple PROTEIN found in the seeds of cereals, such as oryzenin of rice.

Gluten Gluten is a nourishing protein in WHEAT and CEREAL GRAIN, used to make bread dough elastic.

Glycerol see Fatty acids

Glycogen see Carbohydrates, Liver

Glycolysis (gly-KO-sis) The series of chemical reactions in RESPIRATION is called glycolysis. It happens without the presence of free oxygen. Carbohydrates, usually glucose, are changed into pyruvic acid.

The purpose of glycolysis is to release energy for a plant or animal. This is done by breaking the bonds in molecules of food. In plants, such as bacteria, these reactions provide energy and release ethyl alcohol and carbon dioxide. It is a FERMENTATION process.

In animals, such as humans, glycolysis is the formation of lactic acid by muscle cells during work or exercise. These reactions lead to KREBS citric acid cycle which will require the presence of oxygen. H.J.C.

Gnat (NATT) Gnat is a common name for small, biting INSECTS that belong to at least three fly families. All have slim bodies, two large lacy wings, often long feelers, and long legs.

Several varieties of the goat

Those in the gall gnat family sting a plant and make it grow a house for them. Black flies have stocky bodies with humped backs. They are bloodsuckers, often causing the death of livestock. Fungi gnats are mosquito-like and live on fungi, particularly mushrooms.

Gnats have complete METAMORPHOSIS. Some have aquatic larvae. Those in swift streams have adaptations for anchorage. J. C. K.

SEE ALSO: FLY, INSECTA, METAMORPHOSIS

Gneiss see Rocks

Gnu (NEW) Wildebeest is another name for gnu. They are a kind of antelope, lacking the beauty of other antelopes. Gnus are strange in appearance. They have large bison-like heads with long, sad faces. Their bodies and tails are horselike. Horns are smooth and they curl down and then up.

These are large, grazing MAMMALS living in Africa. They travel in large herds of 20 to 50 animals and often cover large distances in search of water. The herds post lookouts who warn of danger by a series of loud snorts.

The gnu (wildebeest) is an African antelope

They gallop like horses, covering ground in long strides. Young are born in the fall. Gnus belong to the family Bovidae. J. C. K.

SEE ALSO: ANTELOPE

Goat Goats are relatives of sheep and belong to the same family as the cow. There are 4½ million domestic goats in the United States. They are useful to man for milk and cheese. In some parts of the world where grass for pasture is scarce and cattle cannot live, they are the chief source of meat, clothing, and leathergoods. The *nubian* goat of northeast Africa serves these many uses. The goat can live on leaves of shrubs and very short grass.

The ancestor of the domestic goat is the IBEX, a mountain goat of the Caucasian range, and the *turgoat* of the Himalayas. From these mountain animals was developed the *Kasmir* of northwest China. This goat grows a coat of soft white fur or wool beneath long, light brown or white guard hairs. This is combed out for making cashmere. The *Angora* goat of Tibet and Turkey was domesticated from the ibex. Its hair is made into mohair.

The *Toggenburg* from Switzerland is the world's best known dairy goat. Its milk is used in making fine cheeses. This is the goat most frequently raised in farming areas, and the most common breed in the United States. The most popular goat for wool production is the Angora.

The domestic goat weighs about 100 to 120 pounds (45.54 to 54.43 kilograms). It is a ruminant, lives on grass and leaves and can forage food where larger animals would not fare too well. A sure-footed climber, it grazes well on hilly land and mountain slopes.

The goat normally gives birth to one young, but often twins and sometimes triplets are born. The male is called a *buck*, the female is a *doe* and the young is called a *kid*.

The rock goat is really the IBEX and the tur. Erroneously the name *rock goat* has been applied to the Rocky Mountain ungulate, which is not a true goat, but a sheep and a relative of the Big Horn. D. C. H.

Goat, the see Capricornus

Goddard, Robert Hutchings (1882-1945) Robert Goddard was an American physicist who is now recognized as the "father of the modern rocket."

When he was only seventeen, Goddard wrote about the possibility of using ROCKETS for interplanetary travel. He was ridiculed and mocked, but by 1916 he had made enough progress to receive a grant from the Smithsonian Institution to continue his researches.

Interrupted by World War I, when he experimented with rockets as weapons, Goddard continued his research on rocket development, and in 1919 submitted a report to the Smithsonian Institution. He suggested the multiple-step principle be used, and he also advised the use of liquid rather than powder propellent.

In 1926 Goddard launched the first successful liquid-fuel rocket. It carried two tanks—one for fuel and one for liquid oxygen needed for combustion—and traveled up to 184 feet (56.08 meters) in two and one-half seconds. Its maximum speed was 60 miles (96.56 kilometers) per hour. Goddard, however, did not make public the news of this flight until 1936, and by that time other scientists had made better rockets. When a German researcher wrote asking for a copy of the Smithsonian report, Goddard sent him one, but beyond that he refused to cooperate with the Germans.

Although Goddard continued his research, he made no outstanding discoveries. He had already made his contribution to scientific history. D. H. J.

Goiter Goiter is an unusual swelling in the neck. The swelling is an enlargement of the THYROID gland, a U-shaped gland found just above the collar bones.

There are three principal varieties of goiter: simple, exophthalmic, and nodular. *Simple* goiter is most frequent and the most interesting, because it is found in certain geographical areas and affects a fairly large number of people. It is found in those areas where the soil and water are deficient in IODINE. This is overcome by adding a small amount of iodine to table salt. The thyroid gland absorbs the iodine from food and water intake and uses it to manufacture, for the body's use, the hormone *thyroxine*. Thyroxine is necessary for the body's growth and well being.

Exophthalmic goiter, also called hyperthyroidism, is a more severe type in which the body poisons itself from an over-secretion of the thyroid hormone. To the enlarged neck are added other symptoms such as prominent eyes, a rapid heart action, and restless overactivity.

Nodular goiter is the name used when none of the previous symptoms are noted but there are certain enlargements in the gland. H.K.S.

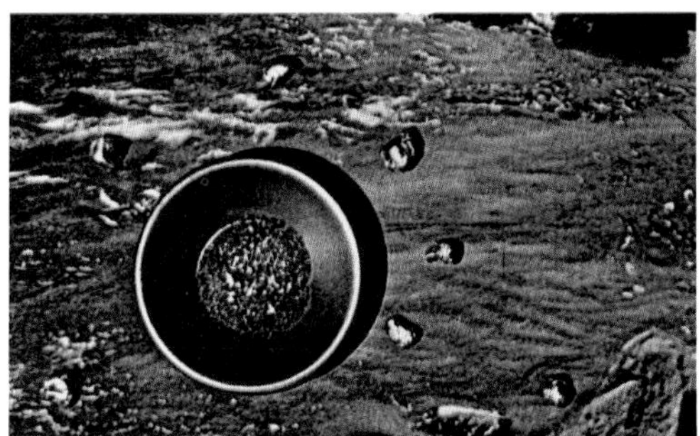

Smithsonian Institution

Panned gold

Gold Gold is a bright yellow metal found in small amounts throughout the world. Pure gold is a chemical element and is a highly prized, precious metal. Because it is scarce and its production costly, the price of gold has always been high compared with other metals. Since it is very soft, it is usually mixed with a harder METAL such as copper or silver. Such a mixture is known as an ALLOY. Pure gold occurs in nature, but it is usually found in goldbearing rocks, or ores, which must be mined.

Smithsonian Institution

Gold in nature and some of man's uses for it

South Africa, Russia, Canada, and the United States produce eighty per cent of the world's gold. The largest mine in the United States, in South Dakota, produces more than sixteen million dollars worth of gold each year. Most of it goes to the U.S. treasury. More gold is used in jewelry and watch-making than in industry. Dentists use gold alloys for fillings and braces. Since gold is not harmful to the tissues, doctors have found it useful. Gold, being soft, can be hammered into extremely thin sheets called *gold foil,* and it can be pulled into the finest wire. Industrially it is used in electric and ELECTRONICS equipment. Pure gold is twenty-four CARAT gold. The number of carats describes how many parts in twenty-four are gold.

In chemistry, gold (symbol Au from the Latin word *aurum)* has atomic number 79. In the same family as copper and silver, its electron ring structure of 2 (in the first shell), 8, 18, 32, 1, shows that it is an excellent conductor of electricity. The one electron in the outer shell "invites" electron flow. Gold has an atomic weight of 196.97 and is more than 19 times as heavy as water. It melts at 1063° C. (1945.4° F.), and boils at 2600° C. (4712° F.). Gold is chemically inactive so it never corrodes, oxidizes, or rusts, and it dissolves only in *aqua regia* (hydrochloric and nitric acids).

H.W.M.

SEE ALSO: ATOM, ELEMENTS

Goldenrod see Wild flowers

Goldfinch The goldfinch is a bright yellow songbird with black wings, tail and cap. Its lilting song gives it another name—*wild canary.* The eastern goldfinch, the most common in North America, is smaller than 5 inches (12.7 centimeters) long. In winter the male turns a brownish-olive colcr, resembling the female and the young.

In early summer the goldfinch builds its nest of fine grasses lined with thistle down. It is usually built 5 to 20 feet (1.52 to 6.1 meters) up in a tree or in a berry bush out of the sun's rays. The three to six eggs are pale bluish-white with no markings. D.J.I.

SEE ALSO: FINCH

Goldfish Goldfish are small ornamental fish belonging to the *carp* family. There are many varieties. Although goldfish appear so frequently in American homes as to seem native, they are descendants of the plain Chinese blue-brown carp. Their many colors and oddities are the result of cross-breeding and artificial selection by man. But even the most beautiful goldfish will revert to type if returned to its wild state. Goldfish come in gold, red, black, white, bronze, gray, brown, orange, striking color combinations and even spotted.

The ancient Chinese first bred goldfish but the Japanese helped produce many of the present day beautiful and fancy types. Goldfish breeding in America began in 1878 in government nurseries.

Goldfish are easy to care for and will reward the careful owner by living 25 years or more. A balanced AQUARIUM not reset more than twice a year is best. Water should be kept clean and it should be cold rather than warm. Warm water and over-crowding causes poor health and appetite in the fish. When uncrowded in a large aquarium or pond, goldfish will achieve a length of 2 feet (.61 meter). Under more crowded conditions they won't grow over 6 inches (15.24 centimeters). In small tanks, goldfish are fed two or three times weekly;

A few of the many varieties of goldfish

daily or six days a week in aquariums that hod over 8 gallons (30.28 liters). A variety of foods in addition to prepared fish foods will keep the fish healthy and active.

About twenty kinds of goldfish are marketed in America. *Fantails* are popular goldfish; *comets* have long forked tails; *Moors* are black; *telescopes* have protruding eyes; *lionheads* have no dorsal fin and have hood-like prominences on the head and scaleless fish have thin scales that are almost invisible. D. C. H.

SEE ALSO: TROPICAL FISH

Goldschmidt, Victor Moritz (1888-1947) Goldschmidt was a Norwegian mineralogist, petrologist, and geochemist who established a new science of inorganic CRYSTAL chemistry. His contributions aided in a better understanding of the chemistry of the earth.

Goldschmidt was the leading figure in establishing the science of *geochemistry,* which deals with understanding the laws that govern rock and mineral development. He applied the then newly-discovered X-ray techniques for determining a mineral's atomic structure. In 1929 Goldschmidt investigated the geochemistry of individual elements. He used quantitative *spectroscopy* for rapid identification of small amounts of many elements with a high degree of accuracy. P.P.S.

Golgi bodies see Cells

Gonad (GOH-nadd) Gonads are either male or female sex glands. The gonad of a male produces sperm and is known as a TESTIS. The gonad of a female produces eggs, or ova, and is known as an OVARY.

Gonads also produce hormones which control the development of secondary sex characteristics. The ovarian hormone, ESTROGEN, brings about the development of female characteristics such as the mammary glands. The testicular hormone, testosterone, an ANDROGEN, influences such male characteristics as the growth of a beard. J.C.K.

SEE ALSO: ENDOCRINE GLANDS, OVARY, REPRODUCTIVE SYSTEMS, STEROID, TESTIS

Gonorrhea This is a VENEREAL DISEASE which affects the membranes, mainly of the genital organs. It is caused by a bacteria *(gonococcus).* It produces a yellowish discharge in a man. A woman may have no symptoms. Urination may be very painful. The infection may settle in joints, producing arthritis.

SEE ALSO: REPRODUCTIVE SYSTEM, SYPHILIS

Googol A googol is the number one followed by 100 zeros, although sometimes it is used to represent any very large number.

Canada geese

Gooseberries resemble large, green grapes

Goose The goose is a large waterfowl. It is so large that its only bird enemy is an eagle. Most geese summer in far northern Canada or the Arctic, and winter in southern United States and Mexico. They eat grasses and grains.

Wild geese may live as long as 30 years. They mate for life. The female nests in a hollow in the ground, using nearby materials and soft down from her breast. She lays as many as 10 eggs which the male (*gander*) helps incubate.

Geese fly definite migration paths in V-shaped formations going as fast as 50 miles (80.48 kilometers) an hour.

The *blue goose* has a striped grayish body with a whitish neck and head. It follows the Mississippi flyway from James Bay in Canada to certain marshes in Louisiana. Blue geese and snow geese often migrate in mixed flocks.

The *snow goose,* a white goose with yellowish markings on its head and neck, breeds in the Arctic regions and winters in southern United States and Mexico.

The *Canada goose* breeds throughout Canada. It winters in Mexico. It is dark grayish-brown with a black neck and head. There are many sizes of Canada goose.

Ross's goose, a rare species, is small and white. It migrates from Canada over the Rockies to Sacramento. E. R. B.

A gopher peers up from snow around its burrow

Courtesy Society For Visual Education, Inc.

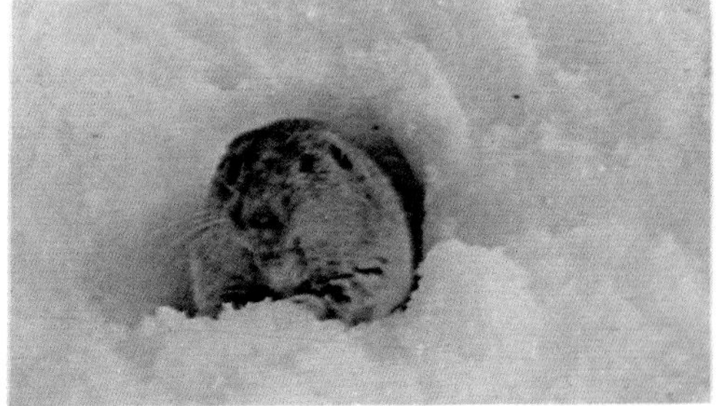

Gooseberry The gooseberry bush is a low shrub. It is very hardy and thrives well in cold climates. The stem may have thorns. The flower is single and the fruit is a true berry.

This plant is native to Europe and Asia and is grown there more than in the United States. It is a member of the *saxifrage* family. The fruit is used in jams and desserts. It can cause damage as an alternate host of the white-pine blister rust.

The *otaheite* gooseberry is a wild tree of another family which bears yellow fruits. These fruits contain so much acid they are not eaten raw but are made into preserves or pickled. H. J. C.

Gopher Gophers are North American gnawing animals or RODENTS. They are medium to small mammals, usually some shade of brown. Gophers have cheek pockets opening on each side of the mouth. These pockets, or pouches, are lined with fur. Front or incisor teeth are large, yellowish, and always seen through the mouth opening. The haired skin of the upper lip passes behind the incisors when the mouth is closed. The tails of gophers are short and have little hair.

Front claws curve as an adaptation for digging. When gophers burrow, they leave fan-shaped piles of earth around the plugged opening. Although gophers are active day and night and do not hibernate, they are seldom seen above the ground.

Gophers feed on roots and TUBERS. Sometimes they gather plants aboveground and drag them underground into their burrows.

Northern species breed once a year; southern ones may breed twice. They belong to the family Geomyidae. Some of the ground squirrels are mistakenly called gophers. J. C. K.

SEE ALSO: RODENT

Courtesy Society For Visual Education, Inc.

Gorillas are difficult to raise in captivity

Gorilla The largest and strongest of the manlike APES are the gorillas. Adult males may weight over 400 pounds (181.44 kilograms), and be 5 to 6 feet (1.52 to 1.83 meters) tall when standing erect. Female gorillas are usually smaller.

They have deep-set eyes under heavy brow ridges, and a face covered with black wrinkled skin. They have wide mouths with large strong teeth. Their bodies are covered with dark brown or black wooly hair that turns gray as they grow old.

Gorillas have long, powerful arms which, when they stand erect, extend to the middle of their knees. They walk on all four limbs or in an upright position. Gorillas have an opposable great toe on each foot which moves like a thumb. This enables them to use their feet for grasping objects as they would their hands.

Some gorillas live in mountain areas, but most live deep in the forests of Africa. They travel through the jungles in small family groups, usually a male, one or two females, and several young gorillas. Unlike most of the other anthropoid apes, gorillas are not tree-dwellers. The young climb a great deal, but as they mature, they spend most of their time on the ground.

Gorillas make fierce sounds, at times resembling a bark, and, at other times, a roar. They often pound their chests and stamp their feet while making loud sounds.

It is very difficult to keep gorillas in captivity. They develop many diseases common to man. It is almost impossible to tame gorillas unless they are captured when very young. The lifespan of gorillas ranges from 20 to 30 years. G. A. D.

SEE ALSO: CHIMPANZEE, GIBBON, LEMUR, MONKEY

Gourds

Courtesy Society For Visual Education, Inc.

Gourd A gourd is a hard-shelled FRUIT which grows on a vine. Primitive people used gourds as dishes and soup spoons. Today gourds are painted bright colors and used for decoration. They are attractive without painting, in their natural colors of green or yellow.

There are two varieties of gourds. The *yellow-flowered* plant has small gourds. The spoon gourd, ladle gourd, nest egg gourd, and bicolor gourd are examples. The *white-flowered* gourd has very large fruits. The bottle gourd, kettle gourd, Hercules club, and dipper gourd are examples.

The vine grows from seed and produces its fruit in the autumn. P.G.B.

Gout Gout is a type of ARTHRITIS causing swelling and inflammation in a joint. The large toe is frequently affected. The pain is intense, sometimes lasting for weeks, with a tendency to recur.

The exact cause of gout is not known, but it seems to run in certain families. Marked changes in the body chemistry, one being an increase in URIC ACID, cause the sodium of the blood and uric acid to form sodium urate. This compound is deposited around the joints, in the cartilage, or frequently in the lobe of the ear. If deposited in the kidneys, it can lead to kidney damage and uremic poisoning.

When gout starts, the joint feels as though a bone were dislocated. If the same joint is repeatedly attacked, it becomes distorted and more or less crippled.

Acute gout attacks are treated with anti-inflammatory drugs and with rest for the affected joint. Between attacks some diet changes are occasionally helpful, but medication can now be taken to lower the level of uric acid in the bloodstream, which prevents the deposits of material *(tophi)* in the skin, joints, and kidneys. H.K.S./E.S.S.

The grackle is found throughout America

Grackle Grackles are large blackbirds with a shiny look to their black feathers. They have long, pointed, black bills, black legs and feet, and yellow eyes. There are three main species of grackles in the United States. Usually they are found in flocks.

The most unusual of the grackles is the boat-tailed. It has a huge, keel-shaped tail that is half the length of the bird. In the south it is called a jackdaw. The female is smaller and brown. Grackles feed on grain, insects, berries, and lizards.

The common purple grackle gleams with iridescent purple colors. It has a long, wedge-shaped tail. Flocks of this species are often found in city parks where they are regarded as pests. In the country, large flocks strip corn and other grainfields.

The bronze grackle is similar to the purple except for their bronze metallic feathers.

Nests are built on platforms of dry weeds. The female jackdaw cares for her young. The purple male grackle guards the eggs. J. C. K.

Four methods of grafting

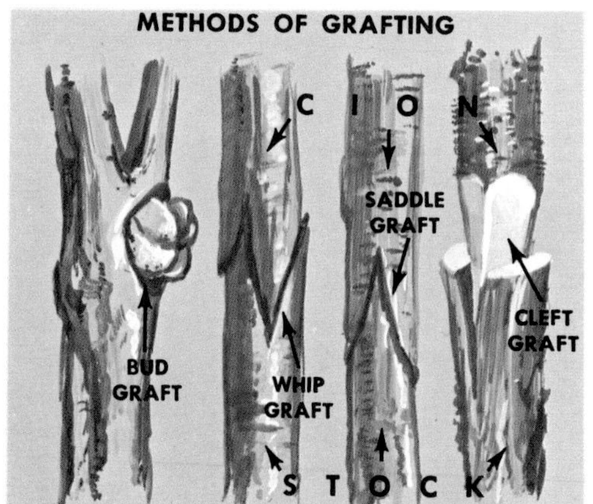

Grafting Grafting is the process of attaching a part of one plant to another plant. The areas of growing cells (CAMBIUM) must be touching each other. The part which is grafted is the *cion*. The rooted plant to which the first plant will be joined is called the *stock*. The cion may be a bud, a small twig, or a piece of a stem.

There are several reasons for this form of propagation (growing new plants). It may furnish the cion with a better root system than its own. Grafting can change the fruit-bearing quality of the stock by substituting a different crown. An apple tree may have several branches grafted to it, enabling one tree to bear a different kind of apple on each branch. Grafting is also used when plants cannot be successfully propagated by division, cuttings, or layering.

The cion and the stock usually belong to the same species. Sometimes two specimens from different botanical families are grafted to produce an odd plant and fruit. The dwarf variety of fruits are produced in this way. Grafting should be done in the winter or spring while the cion is still dormant.

Many methods of grafting have been developed. There are bud grafting, whip grafting, saddle grafting, cleft grafting and others. In all cases it is important that the tissue which lies between the bark and the wood in both the cion and the stock are in contact with each other. After the two parts have been joined, the union is covered with wax and wrapped securely to prevent evaporation and to keep the scion in place.

A wax for covering the open area is made of four parts RESIN, two parts beeswax, one part tallow, and one-half part LINSEED OIL. All of these ingredients are melted together, then poured into cold water to harden. This mixture is then worked and pulled until it becomes tough. For quick application, the liquid wax may be applied with a brush. The wax is kept liquid over a heater. W. J. K.

SEE ALSO: PLANT TISSUES, PROPAGATION

Grain see Barley, Cereal grains, Corn, Grasses, Rice, Rye, Wheat

Gramicidin see Bacteriology

Grand Banks Banks are shallows at or near the outer margins of the continental shelf. The Grand Banks extend from Cape Cod to Newfoundland. The average depth of these banks is about 250 feet (76.2 meters), although much greater depths can be found.

Several theories have been advanced regarding the origin of the Grand Banks. Most agree that they are related to the continental shelf and have been influenced by the last Ice Age. Great quantities of glacial debris, such as gravel and boulders, have been found at considerable depths far from land.

Fog is very typical over the Grand Banks. This occurs where warm, moist air overlying the GULF STREAM is close to the cold Labrador Current. Depending upon wind direction, an advection may be formed. This is one of the foggiest regions of the world. Icebergs are frequent visitors to the northern banks.

The Grand Banks are one of the greatest fishing areas of the world. The shallow depth combined with the mixing of the warm waters of the Gulf Stream with the cold water of the Labrador Current provides an ideal environment for PLANKTON which, in turn, supply ample food for the fish. H. S. G.

SEE ALSO: CONTINENT, CURRENTS, GULF STREAM, OCEAN, OCEANOGRAPHY

Grand Canyon see North America

Granite see Rocks

Granulation Granulation describes what happens when a wound heals. Cells and blood vessels (which look like granules under a microscope) travel from the edge to the center, forming new tissue. A scar can be left.

Grape Grapes are berries that grow in bunches on climbing plants called *vines*. They hold fast, as they climb, with small coiled stems or *tendrils*. Wild grapes are often an important food for animals.

The leaves of the plants are large, single and alternate along the stems. Leaf veins, made of xylem and phloem tubes, enter the leaf at one point and spread out. This arrangement is known as *palmate venation*. Tendrils grow unequally at the tips. Unequal growth enables the tips to move slowly in all directions. If a moving tip touches something solid, such as a trellis, the rate of growth in the tip increases so much that the tendril begins to coil, usually around the solid object. In this way the vine becomes anchored. J. C. K.

SEE ALSO: VINE

Grapefruit see Citrus fruits

Courtesy Society For Visual Education, Inc.

The popular, sweet blue Concord grapes are only one of many kinds of grapes

Graphite Graphite is one of the two crystalline forms of CARBON. The DIAMOND is the other. Graphite is shiny black in color, soft and greasy to touch. Crystals of graphite are thin scales which easily slip and slide over each other. Graphite makes a good lubricant, but its best known use is "lead" pencils. Graphite is also used as a moderator in NUCLEAR REACTORS.

Graphite is a fair conductor of electricity, resists chemical action, and will not vaporize except at very high temperatures. Its many uses include paints, ELECTRODES, electrotyping, and lubricants. V. V. N.

Indian grass, used with others for grazing

Buffalograss, a drought-resistant grass

Grasses Plants belonging to the grass family are probably more important to man than those of any other group of plants. Besides the many grasses of lawns and pastures, man eats many grass seeds and the animals that man uses for food have lived upon grasses. If all grass were to disappear, man and other animals would probably starve to death. Grasses that are grown by man as food for himself and his animals are called *cereals*. There are about 10,000 kinds of grasses, with grass cereals, such as wheat, corn, rice, rye, barley and oats, and sugar cane, being most important to man.

Grasses (family *Gramineae*) belong to the *monocotyledon* group of seed plants. All of the monocot plants have only one seed leaf for nourishment of the embryo. When grasses germinate or sprout, the *cotyledon* or seed leaf never appears above ground. It acts as a "middle man," absorbing food (endosperm) stored in the seed and passing it to the developing embryo.

Grass roots are adventitious and uniformly of the same diameter. When an underground stem or *rhizome* is present, the root system arises from this stem.

Stems of grasses are often hollow except at the nodes and, except for bamboo, are non-woody and short. New branches arise only from the basal nodes close to or slightly below the ground. This type of branching is called *tillering*.

Leaves of grass plants are typical of mono-

Bermuda grass, important in soil conservation

All photos U.S. Department of Agriculture

cots. They are long and pointed, often being enclosed in a basal sheath. Growth occurs at the leaf base. Veins do not form a network throughout the leaf but instead run parallel to one another from the base to the tip.

Grasses bear small flowers with almost no petals or sepals (*perianth*). In place of the perianth, the floral sex organs are covered by papery, leaf-like bracts often called *glumes*. Depending upon the species, single flowers or clusters of them form *spikelets*. These in turn are clustered along a central floral axis or stem. If the central stem puts forth branches that get smaller from base to tip (as in oats), the entire floral cluster is known as a *panicle*. If, as in wheat, the spikelets are directly attached to the main floral axis, the complete cluster is called a *spike*.

The fruit of a grass is usually a grain, called *caryopsis*. In a few cases, as in *dropseed* grass, it is an achene. In a fruit of the grain type, the dry, papery ovarian wall of the flower becomes fused to the seed, thus forming the outer seed coat. An achene is actually a small nut with the dry, hard ovary wall enclosing the seed but not becoming fused with it. J. C. K.

SEE ALSO: CEREAL GRAINS, MONOCOTYLEDON

Grasshopper A grasshopper is an insect that jumps through grass or shrubs on its long hind legs. Most adults have strong wings, and many kinds have green bodies so that they easily hide from birds and other preying animals.

Grasshoppers belong in insect order *Orthoptera*. The *short-horned* grasshoppers, some of which are called *locusts*, have a pair of short antennae; and the female's *ovipositor*, or egg-laying organ, is short. The brown "tobacco juice" they spew out when caught is partly digested grass. Many locust species thrive on man's grain crops.

The less familiar *long-horned* types have thread-like antennae that may extend back beyond their bodies. *Katydids* are in this group, and the males are noted for their rasping calls made from tree hide-outs.

Grasshoppers lay many eggs in holes drilled with their ovipositors, in the earth or in twigs. The eggs are glued together with a sticky secretion

Buchsbaum

A short-horned lubber grasshopper

Buchsbaum

The katydid, a long-horned grasshopper, makes a shrill sound by rubbing its wings together

Female grasshoppers lay rice-grain-shaped eggs, either within grass stems or twigs or —as in common prairie species—in little ground holes bored with their ovipositors. Hatching babies, or *nymphs*, look like miniature adults but have no wings and immature reproductive organs. Grasshoppers have four wings, two front leathery ones and a hind pair used in flying that are transparent or colored.

SEE ALSO: INSECTA D. A. B.

Gravel It is loose deposits of small, rounded, smooth stones and pebbles. Gravel is often found mixed with sand and clay, although pockets of pure gravel are not uncommon. In MEDICINE, gravel is a deposit of small calculous stones in the kidneys or urinary tract.

SEE: CONCRETE

Gravity One of the earliest experiences that people have is that objects fall to the ground if one lets go of them or takes away their means of support. The explanation of this familiar action was a giant step forward for the development of science.

SIR ISAAC NEWTON, famous for his laws of motion, proved that the behavior of the PLANETS and moon in their orbits could be explained by some invisible force which urges or pulls them together. It is said that he was lying under an apple tree and observed an apple falling to the ground. He wondered why the apple didn't go up instead of down. This incident started the investigation which led to the above statement about the planets. His investigations led to some of the greatest advances in the field.

Newton further stated that the same force which keeps the planets in their orbits also causes objects to fall to the ground. He said that this attraction exists between any two masses regardless of their position. The attraction occurs to both masses equally, because the first mass attracts the second mass with the same force as the second attracts the first. Newton called this universal force of attraction *gravitation.*

In 1672 or 1687 (historians are not sure as to the exact year), Newton formulated this statement into a law now called *Newton's Law of Universal Gravitation.* It states that the gravitational force between any two masses is directly proportional to the product of their masses and inversely proportional to the square of the distance separating the centers of mass of the two objects. In algebraic language this reads

$$F \propto \frac{m_1 m_2}{r^2}$$

To make an equation from this one needs a constant of proportionality which Newton

WHERE IS THE CENTER OF GRAVITY ON YOUR BODY?

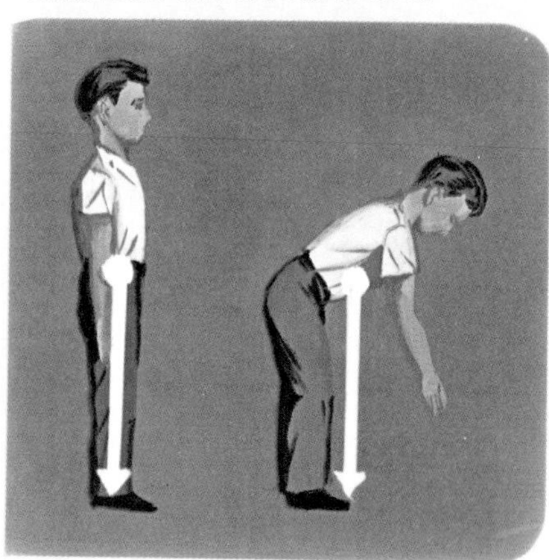

1. **Stand up straight with heels against a wall.**
2. **Where is most of the weight placed in this position?**
3. **Keeping your feet in the same place, bend over and try to touch the floor in front of you.**
4. **Did you change the center of gravity? What happens when you do?**

called *G*. Thus the equation reads

$$F = G\,\frac{m_1 m_2}{r^2}$$

Newton could not determine the value of *G* because the mass of the earth was not known at that time.

In 1797 and 1798, Henry Cavendish measured the attraction between two metal spheres and since all other values were known he could determine the value for G. Recent experiments at the National Bureau of Standards give 6.670×10^{-8} dyne cm^2/gm^2 as the value for G. Knowing this value, one can determine the mass of the earth, sun, moon and other planets. From the value of G, one can see that the force of attraction is small unless one body has a large mass.

The equation shows that the force exerted on a body becomes smaller as the distance between it and the attracting body is increased. Since the earth is quite irregular in shape, one might expect then that the force exerted on a body would vary depending on its position on the surface of the earth. This assumption is correct. For instance, the radius of the earth is some 13

The force of gravity on the moon's surface is six times weaker than the earth's.

miles (20.92 kilometers) more at the equator than at the poles.

The force of gravity which earth exerts on a body is called *weight.* Since the surface of the earth is farther from the center at the equator, the force exerted on a body is smaller, hence it weighs less there than at the poles. Actually, the force due to gravity at the equator is about ½% less than at the poles. In a 180-pound (81.65-kilogram) man this is a difference of about one pound (.45 kilogram). Thus, weight is treated just as any other force with its direction toward the center of the earth. A few values of the ACCELERATION of freely falling bodies for various places in the world are given in the table above. The very small variation in the values from point to point tells that there is no need for concern in everyday living. In scientific work, however, the size of these values is quite important and must be taken into account.

One of the most common examples of the effect of gravitational attraction is given by tides. Although these are most apparent in the OCEAN, they also occur in small lakes and even in the solid earth itself. Tides are

VALUES FOR ACCELERATION OF FREELY-FALLING BODIES FOR SOME PLACES

SAMPLE LOCATION	ALTITUDE	ACCELERATION VALUE
MINNEAPOLIS, MINNESOTA	815 Feet	980.60 $\frac{cm}{sec^2}$
BOSTON, MASSACHUSETTS	11 Feet	980.39 $\frac{cm}{sec^2}$
SAN FRANCISCO, CALIFORNIA	65 Feet	979.97 $\frac{cm}{sec^2}$
NEW ORLEANS, LOUISIANA	5 Feet	979.32 $\frac{cm}{sec^2}$
GREENWICH, ENGLAND	235 Feet	981.19 $\frac{cm}{sec^2}$
ROME, ITALY	66 Feet	980.35 $\frac{cm}{sec^2}$
CAPE TOWN, SOUTH AFRICA	25 Feet	979.66 $\frac{cm}{sec^2}$

✳ THINGS TO DO

DOES THE PULL OF GRAVITY BECOME GREATER THE FARTHER AN OBJECT HAS TO FALL?

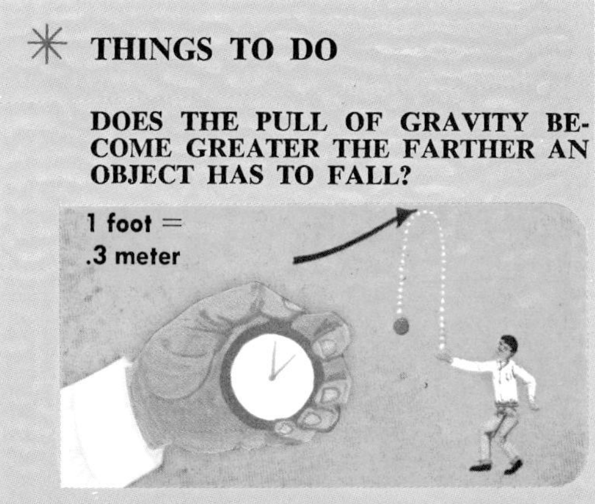

1. **You will need a stopwatch for this experiment and a person who is accurate in throwing certain distances.**
2. **Throw a ball 10 feet (about one story) into the air. At the point where the ball stops and begins to descend start the stop watch instantly. The second the ball hits the ground stop the watch and record the time.**
3. **Repeat the experiment by throwing the ball about twice as high (20 feet up) and again at thirty feet.**
4. **Does the ball fall faster the higher it is thrown?**

caused by the attraction of the sun and moon acting on the earth. Gravitational attraction of the sun and moon, plus the rotation of the earth, makes analysis of the forces causing tides very complex.

Since the earth passes closer to the sun at certain times of the year than at others, one might expect that this plays an important role in gravitational attraction for the earth. Michelson and Gale have found that the rise and fall of the surface of the earth is as much as 9 inches (22.86 centimeters) in the spring of the year around Chicago. This amount was enough to show that the earth is about as rigid as steel.

The earth's atmosphere is also affected by the gravitational pull of the moon and sun. Since the mass of the ATOMOSPHERE is quite small in comparison to the other bodies, the effect is quite small, less than 1/10 per cent of the average air pressure.

A.E.L.

SEE ALSO; FALLING BODIES; FLIGHT, PRINCIPLES OF; FORCES; MOON; TIDES

Great auk see Auk; Birds, flightless

Great Barrier Reef see Australia

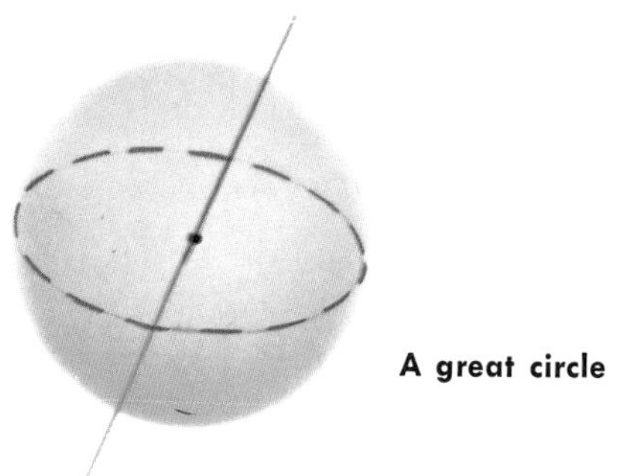

A great circle

Great circle A great circle is any circle on a sphere the plane of which passes through the center of the sphere. It is therefore the largest circle able to be drawn on a sphere. The EQUATOR is one of the earth's great circles.

Great Lakes see North America

Greater Dog see Canis Major and Canis Minor

Grebe (GREEB) Grebes are ducklike water birds. They do not fly well but are fine swimmers and divers. They are mostly gray with markings dependent upon the species.

Out of 25 species, about six are found in the United States. None of them travels very far away from water. Grebe nests are patches of water-soaked vegetation in which three to nine dull white eggs are laid. Many grebes cover nests with wet vegetation if they leave them.

As an adaptation for swimming and diving, they have lobe-toed feet with flat nails instead of webbed feet like the ducks, with whom they are often confused. They also have more pointed bills, seem to lack tails, have narrower heads and necks than ducks, and sit lower in the water. The grebes usually hold their necks erect when they swim. Ducks hold their necks in a slight curve except when they are frightened. J. C. K.

SEE ALSO: BIRD

Pied-billed grebes have bills striped with black

Greenhouse A greenhouse is a glass building in which plants are grown and kept. The greenhouse has many uses: seedlings of plants are protected in the winter, plants are grown from seeds and cuttings, bulbs planted in pots are stored while they are rooting, and plants are grown out of season.

The temperature and humidity in the greenhouse are controlled. Vegetables and fruits can be grown out of season for winter consumption. Salad greens, asparagus, and strawberries in the winter are some of the products of the greenhouse.

There are many types of greenhouses. One kind easily made for the private home can be attached to the home and the heat should be supplied by the house heating plant. It should be fully exposed to the sun and protected from the north and west winds. A separate unit may be built on top of the ground or over a basement.

Hot water and steam heat are used to heat greenhouses. The glass walls and roof let in the natural light of the sun. Ventilation is an important factor. The greenhouse is constructed to let in air when necessary and at the same time to keep out the rain. Ventilation is specially controlled to prevent drafts from blowing directly on the plants.

The amount of water needed varies with the species of plant being cultivated in greenhouses. Many plants are damaged by overwatering. The drainage, the amount of artificial heat, and the type of soil all have a bearing on the amount of moisture required. The plants are watered thoroughly in early morning. Care is taken to protect the tops of plants from water when the temperature is falling.

Plants are protected from insect pests by periodical fumigation of the greenhouse. Calcium cyanide and tobacco preparations are most commonly used.

The greenhouse is equipped with a system of shading. In the winter all the available sunlight is necessary, but in the spring when the sunlight gets stronger the plants need to be protected from the strong rays. White lead mixed with water or gasoline may be applied to the glass with a brush or sprayer. This paint may be removed with stiff brushes when the shade is no longer needed.

Plants such as African violets can be started under white and blue fluorescent lights

Hotbeds and *coldframes* are forms of greenhouses. There are several ways of building and heating hotbeds and coldframes, which must be well insulated to hold in the heat. One way is to dig a hole in the ground. A layer of MANURE is packed down and covered with a layer of soil. A wooden frame is built around the walls of the pit and the top is covered with glass. The walls may also be made of concrete and hot water pipes installed to produce heat. Electric bulbs can be used to heat hotbeds. The light from the bulb stimulates growth in plants. During cold weather straw or mats are used to cover the glass tops to keep in the heat. The hotbed is used to start plants early. The coldframe, which is similarly constructed but heated by the sun, is used to start plants later, closer to the regular planting season.

The *conservatory* is a special greenhouse where plants that have been grown and cultivated elsewhere are displayed.

Some vegetables and fruits are grown out of season in greenhouses known as *forcing houses*. Asparagus, rhubarb, and strawberries are among vegetables grown this way so that people can enjoy them in the winter. The *warmhouse,* which is the warmest part of the greenhouse, is used to produce tropical plants.

Today aluminum is used to construct the frame of the greenhouse. It is particularly desirable because it is rustproof and requires no painting. Glass fiber is substituted for glass. W. J. K.

SEE ALSO: CONSERVATORY; FUMIGANTS; GARDENING; INSECTICIDES; PLANTS, TROPICAL

Greenhouse effect This term is used to describe what happens when the earth's atmosphere traps heat energy from the sun. The phrase is used because air functions like the window glass of a greenhouse. If it were not for the greenhouse effect, the average temperature of the earth would be much colder than it is.

The sun's visible light rays pass through the atmosphere to the earth. The visible light heats the earth. The earth radiates the heat as longer infrared rays. Water vapor and carbon dioxide and other gases in the atmosphere absorb some of the infrared waves before they can escape into space. As the light energy is absorbed, the gas molecules are heated, eventually warming the atmosphere as a whole.

The burning of FOSSIL FUELS and other activities related to a growing worldwide population may be changing the balance of certain gases in the earth's atmosphere. Included are carbon dioxide and other trace gases such as methane, nitrous oxide, and ozone. Each of these gases absorbs ultraviolet rays and helps produce a greenhouse effect. A family of artificial gases called CFC's, used in air conditioners and refrigerators, has been released into the atmosphere for the first time during the twentieth century. CFC's also help produce a greenhouse effect.

Many scientists believe that the earth's greenhouse effect is growing stronger. That condition could lead to *global warming,* a situation which might create serious problems for human beings over much of the planet. Even a modest increase in global temperatures could create severe droughts in some areas, higher ocean levels and therefore flooding in other areas, violent weather patterns, and other uncertain consequences. Because the earth's BIOSPHERE is complex, however, it is difficult to predict the exact consequences of global warming due to the greenhouse effect. Scientists sometimes disagree over the consequences of increases in greenhouse gases. A.J.H./J.H.

SEE ALSO: FOSSIL FUELS, ATMOSPHERE

Greenwich time see Time Zones

Grenade see Bombs, Explosives

Gristle see Cartilage tissue

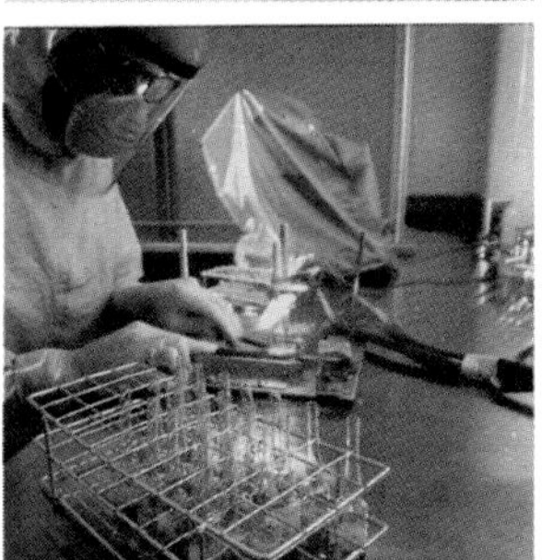
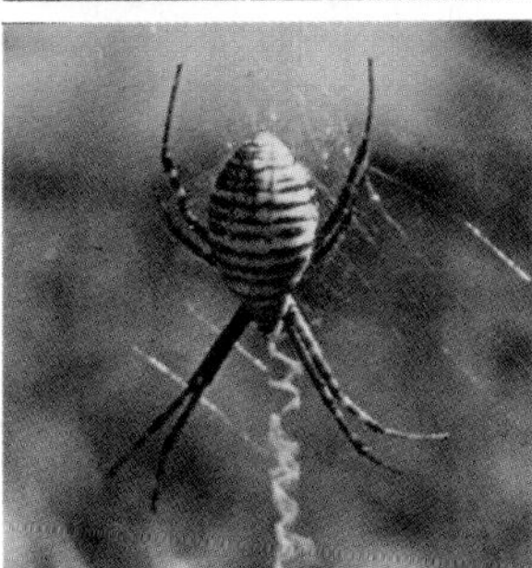

Conversion Factors to Metric Measurement

Length
1 inch = 25.4 millimeters (mm) exactly
1 inch = 2.54 centimeters (cm) exactly
1 foot = 0.3048 meters (m) exactly
1 yard = 0.9144 meters (m) exactly
1 mile = 1.609344 kilometers (km) exactly

Area
1 square inch = 6.4516 square centimeters (cm^2) exactly
1 square foot = 0.092903 square meters (m^2)
1 square yard = 0.836127 square meters (m^2)
1 square acre = 0.404686 hectares (ha)
1 square mile = 2.58999 square kilometers (km^2)

Cubic Measure
1 cubic inch = 16.387064 cubic centimeters (cm^3) exactly
1 cubic foot = 0.0283168 cubic meters (m^3)
1 cubic yard = 0.764555 cubic meters (m^3)

US Liquid Measure
1 fluid ounce = 29.5735 milliliters (ml)
1 fluid ounce = 0.2957 deciliters (dl)
1 pint = 0.473176 liters (l)
1 gallon = 3.78541 liters (l)

US Dry Measure
1 pint = 0.550610 liters (l)
1 bushel = 35.2391 liters (l)

Weight
1 grain = 0.0647989 grams (g)
1 ounce = 28.3495 grams (g)
1 pound = 0.453592 kilograms (kg)
1 short ton = 0.907185 metric tons (t)
1 UK ton = 1.01605 metric tons (t)

Temperature
To convert Fahrenheit to Centigrade (Celsius) complete the following equation. $(F^\circ - 32) \times 5 \div 9 = C^\circ$